Common Threads

A Memoir

Kathie Staniec

Published by Argyle Street Stories
Copyright © 2018 by Kathie Staniec

ISBN-13: 978-1987698879
ISBN-10: 1987698878

Edited by Hunter Moreno

Cover: Reincke, Arno B. *Chicago, Central Business Section*. Chicago, 1916. Map.
https://www.loc.gov/item/76693072
6814 West Argyle Street, Casey and Sunny Weglarz

Printed in the U.S.A.

Contents

Introduction

This is my memoir: the truth as I recall it. Some memories are embedded in my mind as perfect truth or not so perfect truth, but I left them alone because I may have been too young at the time to fully understand. I relayed my story as accurately as I could from historical research, my own memories and the memories from my family and others. My story, however, results from my having been an intensely observant girl stitching together the fragile threads of sadness and joy, interwoven with the hopes, fears and triumphs of the lives of three generations of women...

1

Moving From Chicago To California
Moments at the crossroad of my life

Late August 1982, I felt broken, but somehow it felt like it was meant to be. Up to this day, I had never been adventurous. I had always been comfortable with the things that I was used to, only coloring between the lines with the classic Crayola colors. I was somewhat timid and afraid of things that were different or new. Now, I was on a frightening unknown path that others in my family had experienced; yet I never anticipated just how unsettling it would feel. It was my turn now. I'd been numb since my beloved husband, or sometimes not so beloved husband, lost his job for the third time since we married. So I found myself looking out the window of our old blue Chevy station wagon, loaded with three year old Kevin sitting in the far back third seat and his brother Ryan, a very grown up six year old in the middle. They were surrounded with pillows, games, books, coolers with snacks and suitcases of clothes. Each boy had their favorite stuffed animals, Curious George, Snoopy, etc. for comfort. I could hardly see them back there because of all that was packed around them.

With all that was squeezed into this small space, I almost could picture the final outcome with me sitting in a rocking chair tied to the top of the car like the Beverly Hillbillies, watching the world go by. Sadly, all humor aside, my heart felt like a rock. It was another hot and sticky Chicago summer day as we hit the road and started our journey. The farther west we traveled, I could smell the freshly cut farmland grass as we began our drive along the famous Route 66 from Chicago to Los Angeles, the City of Angels, our final destination. We sure could have used some heavenly support from angels with the way things had been going for us. Maybe this was meant to be, and I had to put my trust in God to direct us down the right path because any other options were slim to nothing.

The moment I dreaded most in my life so far was over, saying goodbye to my parents and sister. My sister kept patting me on the arm saying, "You're going to be OK, I packed cookies and made sandwiches, all of your favorites, for the trip." My dad was ever silent with his jaw muscles straining trying not get emotional, but his sad brown eyes expressed all of his pent up feelings. My mother fluttered around like a caged bird, nervous and worried for us, as she tried not to cry. We drove away with tears in our eyes and lumps in our throats.

I knew that I had to stay strong and act like we were embarking on some sort of great adventure for everyone involved, but inside I felt like I was shattered into tiny little pieces. Somehow, I forced myself to think of a distraction to keep the boys from crying as they watched their loving grandparents disappear in the distance behind us until they were tiny pin dots in the landscape.

I knew what they were feeling, and it really hurt. There was no other choice though. We go where there is work, and so it was. There was nothing but miles of flat green prairie and farms on either side, everyone was getting tired of counting cows after reaching 52 of them with nothing but more of the same to come.

In a desperate attempt to make things better, we played a rousing game of I Spy, and I kept the mood light by pointing out anything and everything of interest to everyone. I was sure the guys were tired of hearing my voice. Finally, the boys in the back were getting drowsy. I was so darn tired after the last few weeks of packing and garage sales that whittled down our possessions to one truckload that contained each of our lives combined. I kept reminding myself to take heart knowing that we were going to a new job for

Glenn. I knew I was not the only one to ever leave everything I know and love to start over in a new place. I felt the changes beginning deep down in me already like tiny seeds in the dark beginning to sprout.

As the trusty co-pilot on our adventure, I pulled out my travel bag and checked our hopelessly unruly paper maps. It was open, fold, crease, and fold the stiff crinkly paper again, while I studied the wiggly yellow highlighted lines snake across the map. My eyes wandered, and tucked into the side pocket, I noticed a carefully folded old-fashioned hanky that my Grandma Carrie gave to me. It was one of many that I saved over the years, and I thought it would bring me a little bit of good luck. It was never used to simply blow my nose. There are throw away tissues for those messy jobs, an invention that is a perfect example of our throw away society. For me, the hanky was just in case I shed a few salty tears and needed to blot them away, but it mostly gave me comfort. This one was white with a beautiful lace border that I carried at my wedding. It had been washed many times and softly worn. I had tucked it into my purse for each of my son's Christenings.

Looking down at my hands holding it, I was reminded of my mother's hands and her mother's before her. Hands that cooked, cleaned our homes, and soothed our babies. My Grandma Carrie would crochet for hours making lace from the finest threads into patterns as diverse as her life. Each thread twisting and turning, backward and forward, with the wisdom of the pattern flowing strong and steady. Grandma had given me countless hankies over the years with borders of her hand crocheted lace. Just thinking of her gave me a peaceful moment, remembering. As I sat back, I held it in my hands and looked out the window again. I finally relaxed and let the memories flow over me. I gently smoothed out the lace border and thought of how often we catch moments in the threads of our lives and stitch them together making lace of our memories, hopes, and dreams.

2

Looking Back

Remembering Grandma Carrie

As we were driving west on that monotonous road we had never traveled before, I began to remember another hot Chicago August day in 1959. Grandma Carrie rode out by bus from the city to visit us every few weeks in summer. We picked her up at the end of the line at Milwaukee Avenue to bring her home with us. The lumbering smelly bus would pull up to the curb and off would step Grandma. Sometimes in her arms she would have a tall, stiff bunch of bright colored Gladiola flowers wrapped in humble newspaper from the flower shop at the end of the bus line to bring to my mom. Other times, she brought a brown paper shopping bag full of something she had made in her kitchen. She would always have a hopeful smile to greet us happily as we pulled over to pick her up.

On one particular visit, the air was heavy with summer as Grandma and I walked together through the front yard of our house with grass so green and fresh. The purple blossoms of Clematis framed the door around us as we stepped into the house. My senses were filled with the sounds and scents of the day. All of the doors and windows were wide open with a soft breeze flowing through the screens. The buzzing sound of lazily flying bumblebees and an occasional distant lawn mower punctuated the peacefulness. Grandma and I sat down side by side in the living room, and I watched her as she gazed out the window seemingly in another place and time. I asked her, "Grandma, can you tell me about what it was like when you were a little girl?" Then with a nod of her head, she began to tell me her story in the soft Polish accent she brought here from her other life.

"I was born in spring on May 16th, 1894 and life in Poland was so different than how you live now," she began. "We had horses and a wagon to get into town. Ours was a small farming village in Poland, and we grew what we needed to eat and traded with other farms what we didn't have. No electric lights, the bathroom was outdoors with a rough wooden seat (really cold in winter), not a nice toilet like we have today. Water was pulled from a well outdoors. When I was very young, about your age, I helped by working on the farm. Everyone chipped in. I didn't go to school and could only read and write a little in Polish that my

Mama taught us. My mother taught my sisters and me how to cook and crochet lace with thread. She also taught us how to sew and we made most of our own clothes. But I loved making lace and practiced whenever I had time to do it.

"One day, the Russians took over our town in Poland. They changed the name of the town and wanted everyone to speak Russian only, so we had to learn Russian. We had to give some of our crops to the soldiers, and we had less to eat. Our lives were full of hard work and fear of the Russian soldiers.

"One cold and muddy Sunday in springtime, my family was attending Holy Mass, each praying for the Blessed Virgin Mary to protect us and give a sign as to what we could do to keep our families safe. Suddenly, Russian soldiers crashed through the huge wooden church doors with their rifles pointing at us and rode their horses into the aisle and right up to the altar. My heart was pounding in fear. The leader told everyone to leave the church. It would no longer be open to us.

"I can still remember how those soldiers' horses dragged all the mud and horse manure right up to the altar and we were pushed and shoved out into the street with guns in our faces.

"They arrested our beloved priest and took him away and chained the massive doors shut. Everyone was crying, because then we knew things would never be the same again. We would not be safe anymore, because the Russians wanted all the men and boys to be soldiers in the Russian army. They told us if anyone refused, they would just be shot. We knew they meant business because they had already shot people who disobeyed their orders."

Then, I stopped her in horror. "Grandma, is this a true story? I can't believe this!" She looked at me with her deep brown eyes and sadly said, "Kathy, I swear to God." She used the Polish word Boje, meaning God. "It's really true. This really happened to us." Then she continued, "I don't like to talk about this to anyone about the old country because it was very hard for us at the time. Everyone in the town was afraid of being arrested themselves, so they all went to their homes to think of how they could get to safety and freedom.

"We were so blessed to have an uncle who had gone to America years earlier, so my Mama and Papa put together a hopeful plan to risk the dangerous and costly trip and move the family to safety. After all, they had been told that in America, if you worked hard, everything was possible. After much whispering, worrying, and planning, it was decided that my Papa, Jozef, would travel alone to America and work for our uncle on their farm in La Salle,

Illinois. It seemed to us that America was on another planet, and not one of us spoke English. We worried, but Papa went.

"Once there, he worked and saved enough money and borrowed the rest to send to Mama who got us ready to go. My brothers and sisters and I each knew we would leave behind almost all that we had. Besides Stella, my older sister, and me there was my brother Adam, aged ten, sister Franczska (Francis) who was seven, Franczek (Frank) a sturdy five year old, and the baby Jozef, three years old.

"When we knew it was time to go, Mama packed only what each of us could carry. My older sister, Stella and I helped her with what we could and had to keep all of the younger children together on the trip and keep them safe, so we clung to each other traveling first by train which we had never done before. Mama, Stella, and I took turns carrying Josef to the train. Then we finally made it to the port in Bremen, Germany, and we boarded the steamship S.S. Bremen on July 4th 1908.

"We heard from other passengers that it was a day that America celebrated independence. Maybe it would bring us good luck. I was about twelve years old then. About the same age as you are now, Kathy. Baby Jozef was so afraid of the boat and all the strangers pushing at each other as they tried to form lines for food and water. He cried a lot and so did Mama, which made us feel bad too.

"The ocean was very rough and the boat rolled from side to side. All we had was $10.00 in American money that Mama hid in her underwear and a few sacks of clothing along with a small box of Mama's treasures from our old house. That's all we had left of our old life.

"The conditions on the steamship were shocking to Mama considering how much they had to pay for passage, but there was *no turning back now*. The smells were bad, the food was bad, and many of us were sick. All we could do was pray. I never forgot the day we finally sailed into New York harbor, July 15th! Everyone on deck went to one side of the boat and cheered and shouted with happiness when they saw Lady Liberty and then grew silent in thought as they began to cry. We all did too. Our home, all of our familiar friends, and our precious family members were so far behind us now, and we probably would never see them again.

"Well, we finally got off the boat in America where we could be safe and free from fear. We had to go to (what she called) Alice Island before we could go to New York City. Everything was so big and exciting and so loud. The people in charge were very helpful to us and said, "Welcome to America" and that's why I named my first baby girl Alice."

I remember trying to tell Grandma a couple of years later, that the island was really called Ellis Island, spelled with an "E", but she never did learn to read or write English. So she corrected me right back to "No, Kathy, ALICE, just like I named my first daughter!" She stuck to her pronunciation and that spelling her whole life in memory of her first American experience. I never tried to correct her again for fear of that stubborn gleam in her eye, but that stubbornness had gotten her through so much in her life and I was always in awe of her!

So, back to Grandma's story. "After we finally arrived at our new home in LaSalle, Illinois, together again with Papa, we started life over. The town had other people from Poland and from some other countries, and my younger brothers and sisters went to school to learn to read and write English. My older sister and I worked to help the family. During that time, my Mama had another baby girl and she was baptized Charlotte, our first American baby." Then Grandma looked deep into my eyes as if she had a big secret, "Kathy, did you know that I have the same first name as your father? His name is Casimir, but being born a girl, I was named Kazimiera. My last name was Rachwalska, but when I came to America, I changed it like everyone else did. When I came to America, I became Carrie Rafalski, an American girl."

As for me, after hearing that first story and the other stories Grandma Carrie shared with me over the years, I listened and continued to learn many things. One single life had evolved so often over the years, beginning with a shy young Polish girl Kazimiera Rachwalska who became American girl, Carrie Rafalsky. Then she was Katie Kusczynski a married woman and mother of three sons, who then sadly became a bereft divorcee. Finally the woman that I knew best and loved most, she became Carrie Happel, a wife once again and mother of seven girls and eventually grandmother to seventeen and great grandmother to forty-one children. I began to see how her life two generations before mine was so full of hardship and yet somehow she accepted the challenge, changed what she could without complaint, and continued to live life with a sense of humor and as gracefully as possible. What a beautiful legacy for me to discover as I skipped, tripped, and trudged my own way through life.

I can still picture Grandma in her later years, sitting in her rocking chair with the golden light from her kitchen window illuminating her hands moving non-stop as she held her gleaming silver crochet hook in her fingers. It was so important to her that she had something to offer her grandchildren and guests with her love. Nearby on the Formica topped kitchen table was a basket containing threads of many colors along with some of her little treasures, her favorite holy cards with pictures of Jesus, Mary, and the saints (some printed in Polish) that she looked at regularly. Most of them were memorial cards to remind her of those she loved that sadly were departed. In a twisted rubber band was a stack of school photos of her numerous grandchildren that she would proudly show any one who would stop by for a visit. After each of her six remaining daughters grew up and got married, her purpose in life began to change. Her job raising them was finally completed. She was poor as a church mouse and, in later days, also an invalid. She had limited use of her legs due to arthritis and other physical ailments, but now she could devote her time to rocking in her chair as she continued to crochet her lace. She looked forward to time spent with each of her children as their ever-growing families came to visit her. Each year was marked with the births of new generations of grandchildren and great grandchildren. She would always listen with interest to them when they shared their latest stories as the years passed by.

Just picturing her in her corner of the kitchen, I felt she was sending me a message to give me strength as I embarked on the most difficult journey of my life as our car continued westward along the miles. Her world had eventually shrunken to only that little space in the kitchen after the years and miles of changes she had experienced and yet, she always seemed so contented. I could almost smell the sweet scent of her talcum powder and feel her embracing me in her soft, cushy hugs. "Well, look who's here!" she would always exclaim. "Go get my shoebox off the shelf." To which I would dutifully go and bring it to her.

Inside were dozens of hankies that she took such pride in for me to choose "just one." Each border of lace was different in tone and hue, some stitches with a different pattern here and there to link the design together. She had always found ways to keep her hands and mind busy, so she would crochet lace almost every day of her life until arthritis twisted her fingers beyond movement and her eyesight began to fail her. It became her quiet comfort while lost in her many memories of years gone by.

3

Back On The Road To California Again, 1982
Our journey continues…

"No turning back…No turning back…" I got
jolted out of my reverie right back to the present, into
the front seat of my big blue Chevy Wonder Wagon
with "Mom, Mom, are we almost there yet?" Kevin
called for the 3rd time as only a three year old can. I
answered, "Almost to the rest stop, Kevin, just a few
more miles." I didn't have the courage to explain that
we had another 1500 miles to go. Then, after another
20 miles Kevin's thin little voice from the back said,
"My tummy doesn't feel good." Oh joy, the dreaded
motion sickness. It was time for another long trip
break. Instead of putting pedal to the metal, we
decided it was safer to stop more often at gas stations
or truck stops for potty breaks and check out their
lovely (in my dreams) bathrooms along the way. Most
of them certainly could have used some TLC. Nothing
like a little guy looking around and hanging back with
a desperate expression saying, "Mommy, I can't go in

here, yuck!" That's when all my motherly coaxing skills came in handy. Then it was back to the car to continue slowly crossing the country at the pace of a turtle. On the road again, we kept pushing ahead across fields as flat as pancakes.

I began to play the "Glad Game" in my mind as Pollyanna always did. I saw the movie Pollyanna when I was quite small and one thing her father taught her before he died stuck out in my mind. Whenever something happens to be sad about, you have to hunt for the glad things or positive aspects to look at and that will help you get through anything. I could picture how hard it must have been for Grandma and her family in steerage, crossing miles of choppy ocean with everyone seasick and going at speeds much slower than we were going as we drove through the country. She and her family made it to America, and we would make it to our destination too. At least we had rest stops and motels along the way. Thank God we had the radio to listen to with the local stations playing familiar songs like the boys' favorite "Eye of The Tiger" to "Ebony and Ivory" by Paul McCartney and Stevie Wonder, my favorite.

The further west we went, the music got more country with "Through The Years," that Kenny Rogers ballad. Songs got even twangier with Willie Nelson and "Always On My Mind," and many other songs of his as the miles went by. After two rounds of "Blue Moon with Heartache" by Roseanne Cash, I had finally had it and I sat up and turned off the radio because there were no other stations to choose from as we drove from one small town through another. Finally, we were only nine hundred miles from the California border and up early after another night at a creepy Motel 6, or 7, or 8.

Now the scenery was really starting to change. All around us was desert, dotted with red rock sculptures in the distance. Then, fields of dry brown brush growing upward through angled foothills as we travelled west. It was so hot and dry, and the sun burned down on us. I can only imagine how hard it was driving in wagon trains rumbling across this no-man's land. Those poor pioneers! No wonder so many of them died on their trip across the country. We rest-stopped here and there to take a few photos, but no camera could capture the bleak beauty of the land.

We were heading toward our final stretch of our journey and took a slight detour to Sun City, Arizona. We were invited to stay with my Auntie Chris and Uncle Don to visit and rest and have some home cooked meals. It was so good to be comforted by them. They were not related by blood, but anyone close to your parents traditionally became Auntie and Uncle. They knew how hard a move of this distance could be, and they were happy to be there for us and we were happy and grateful to be there with them. It was like coming to an oasis in the midst of a desert, quite literally.

When we finally hit the road again toward the last leg of the journey of around 155 miles to the California border, we all began to sing "California Here We Come" over and over in a mix of happy off-tune voices. The isolation of long stretches had mesmerized our senses as we drove along the last leg of our long journey. Once we saw that sign crossing over the state line, everything began to look suddenly brighter.

With a sigh, I sat back and began daydreaming again about the sheltered childhood of my past with so many aunts and cousins always close by and busily interfering in everyone's lives. A nostalgic smile started from my heart and went to my lips. What a raucous bunch! Constant talking, laughing, interrupting, and teasing each other was always the order of the day. We sang together, cried together, and laughed at everything else. We were a really close little cluster of a family! I realized then that those memories were now written into my past to be held and pressed close to my heart, for I knew that I was the next in line to leave home and now my life would never be the same.

4

Remembering Those Happel Girls

My earliest recollections about our big family were what I heard when I was a sneaky little shadow of a girl. I remember so many days sitting just around the corner from the kitchen table at Grandma's house just out of their sight, trying to be invisible so I could listen to Grandma and the Aunties' conversations without them shooing me away. I was the second eldest girl cousin of a whole line of us and took my responsibility to heart. From the time I became eight and each year following, I already felt that I was part of an exclusive club of women and tried to put all of the mysterious pieces of their world into a picture of what it would be like to be grown-up. I learned it was not just all high heels and lipstick.

Once her little chicks were all grown and out of the house, Grandma Carrie lived with Auntie Nancy, the youngest Happel girl, and Uncle Ron and their three children "the 3 R's"—Ronnie, Randy, and Roxanne. It was *the* place to meet for holidays, birthdays, or any other day we just needed a visit with Grandma. Give those Happel sisters a cup of coffee and a piece of coffee cake and then they talked to each other about *everything* and anything, some things too mature even for my innocent ears. I learned what a wild and crazy patchwork quilt families could be.

As the matriarch, Carrie encouraged her girls to grow into independent, self-sufficient women. She set the bar high with her hard working example. She was never a complainer and always tried to provide the best she possibly could. Her daughters always teased Ma that they never saw her sleep. She was up before them and went to bed way after them during all of their growing years. The Happel girls inherited a little from each of their parents' personalities and work ethic. They certainly were a dramatic mix of personalities but somehow everyone fit together closely, just like the old fashioned Russian Matryoshka dolls. Starting with the first brightly painted folk doll that when opened, another smaller doll, containing another doll, and inside a little smaller doll and so on until the last tiny doll the size of a fingernail was revealed. Each doll resembled the next but with different colors and patterned dresses.

In those days, every street kid, and that's what they were, had nicknames. The Happel girls were, Alice, (Al or Lee), Florence (Flossy), Lillian (she died too young), Evelyn (Sunny), Lorraine (Lor), Dolores (Dee Dee), and Nancy (Pisspot, because she was always crying) lived in a girls' world. They were babies of the Depression. They lived on Chicago Avenue or wherever Carrie could afford to shelter that small tribe of women, but Ada Street eventually became the home turf for those Happel girls. And as they married, they stayed right near there within shouting distance of each other.

They always lived on the second or third floor in a three flat because the rents were cheaper the higher you lived. Each block was lined with similar houses leaning shoulder to shoulder. There was just a narrow, dark gangway between each building where the sun didn't shine, but the dirt and trash sure settled.

Combining the memories of some of the sisters, I learned that on Ada Street so many families lived so close in such a little space that everyone seemed to know what everyone else was up to. They gossiped and you knew who was arguing about what. The mothers kept an eye on each other's kids. Motley Elementary School was right across the street and slightly down the block. It was a dark, old brick building with black wire mesh outside the windows to keep anyone from breaking in or anyone from sneaking out. Everyone in the whole neighborhood went to school there. Halfway down the street was

Ciocia Annie's Candy Store (Ciocia is Polish, meaning Auntie and pronounced Cha Cha), and that was every kids paradise because even if you couldn't afford a penny candy, you could look in the glass case, sticky with fingerprints, as long as you wanted and you could watch the few lucky kids with a penny or two take their time choosing just the right piece of sugary delight.

On the street, there was sometimes wagon traffic pulled by a horse (in later years, a small truck replaced each wagon) selling fresh vegetables, bread or ice. When the iceman came, Ma would holler down to him to bring up one block of ice for her little wooden ice box. One of the girls would beg for ice chips from the iceman on hot days in summer and sit on the front porch to suck the cool goodness until it melted. What a treat that was, and they shared with their sisters like they shared everything else. They would pass the ice chip for a lick or two to each little girl who waited expectantly, sitting on the front steps. Life was difficult in those days, but everyone was used to that way of life in a poor neighborhood. As children, they didn't know any other way.

Their flat only had heat from a coal stove in the dining room, which was the middle room, but that room was used for sleeping. They all shared beds, more than two to a bed in spoon formation which meant one had their head on the pillow at the top of the mattress and the next one's head at the foot of the bed and so on filling the bed neatly. Sharing was a way of life back then. Even as they got older if one of the girls had a graduation or a hot date they would pool together everything that they had that was nice and share with each other. Florence had a nice blouse, Alice had a pretty necklace, Sunny had a blue dress, and Lorraine had a sweater with buttons, so somehow they always managed to feel special.

Each of them had chores and watched after their younger sisters while Ma worked. The sisters took turns carrying coal up the stairs from the man next door to keep the flat warm in winter. Every morning, Ma would get up early and add a few coals to get the heat started before the girls would have to get up to go to school or work. There was only cold water, so when you needed hot water for laundry, you would have to boil water on the stove and pour it into a big tin tub. Then, you would scrub the dirty clothes with a long bar of brown laundry soap over a washboard made of wood and corrugated tin. Then rinse everything and dump out the dirty water in the sink or into the yard and twist and wring out the water from the clothes. Then you had to hang them with wooden clothespins on a double clothesline with a squeaky pulley off of the back porch and all the way across the yard.

Along the backs of buildings, all the neighbors could see crossing laundry lines of clean clothes (or sort of clean) strung out over the yards to dry. During winter, it took forever for clothes to dry, and they would have to be hung around the coal stove inside to thaw out because the wet clothes would freeze on the line. On bath days, maybe once a week, they would fill the same big tin tub mixing boiling and cold water and take turns using the same bath water to wash themselves before Ma dumped it out. They were so fortunate to have a toilet in their coldwater flat, but when each of the Happel girls married and moved out, it was to an upstairs flat or a three story across the street with a bathroom in the hallway to share with another apartment. My mom, Sunny, was the only one who moved a few blocks away when she first got married and almost everyday, guess where she took me on the bus to? To Ada Street, of course, and many of my earliest memories are there with all the Happel sisters, Grandma and my new cousins, as each one was born.

As I heard their stories over the years I learned, when each of them graduated from grammar school it was time to get a job. "Ma," my Grandma Carrie, had two jobs. One was at The Pierogi House making that Polish delicacy, and she also worked at Junior's, a banquet hall that served food for weddings and parties.

They served good old-fashioned Polish food and many a night after working in the kitchens, Ma came home with a grocery bag with leftovers to feed her girls. She also baked pies and sold them to neighbors to make ends meet. Ma was a really good cook and had perfected many of her own recipes but especially for homemade sausage and sauerkraut with chopped apples, bacon and onion in it. Her Pierogies were the best, and she would spend a day in the kitchen rolling tender dough and filling those tasty little pockets. When Ma was working at Junior's Hall, if they weren't helping her with food, sometimes the girls would pretend that they knew the people at the wedding or party and join in with the fun and dancing.

They all dreaded market day with Ma. She would take one of the girls to the butcher for a chicken, and she would walk up to the butcher and pick out a chicken clucking angrily from a crate. They would get it by the feet and take it to the back room, and the girls would hear a solid *thunk* as the hatchet cut off their heads. Then, the girls would take it wrapped up in newspaper back home to watch Ma pluck out the feathers, clean it, and cut it up so she could start cooking. Yuck, that's one memory they could do without.

As kids the girls never went to the dentist or doctor unless something was really bad. Instead home remedies to ailments were passed on from family to family or neighbor to neighbor. They couldn't afford to be sick. Babies were born at home without a doctor. Another woman (midwife) from the neighborhood would help out. It was not uncommon for people to die at home with their family all around. One very sad time they always remembered was when the little Happel family was at the beginning stage, with only four daughters born at that time. They went to the park and Pa was going to take Alice and Florence for a rowboat ride on the little lake. Ma stayed on the shore with the baby Evelyn, and with Lillian who was almost three years old at the time and didn't feel good. When Pa got back, the family had to go home immediately because Lillian suddenly had a high fever. They went home and Ma put her to bed. The family hoped and prayed she would get better, but sadly she didn't. Her fever got higher and by morning she died. When other neighbors heard that one of the Happel girls had died, some of them came over to be with us and bring food and bread.

Whenever the Happel sisters spoke of their father, they always did so with love in their eyes. Stefan (Steve) was a musician who also was a chauffeur to make extra money. He tried to work as much as he could to feed his ever growing brood of little chicks, but he was a dreamer and was gone so much of the time. The girls said "When he was home, he entertained us all by singing Russian ballads and playing the harmonica and balalaika, which was his specialty. He taught us Russian folk dances." Those Happel girls loved him unconditionally and always waited for him to be at home, which was so seldom. What a dramatic and talented man he was!

He was born on August 22, 1895 in Kwasnikovko, Russia. When he was 16, he and his father, Dmitry, immigrated to America on September 25th on the steamship S.S. Dominion that left from Liverpool, England. After docking in Philadelphia, Pennsylvania on October 7th, 1912 they went on to Michigan to meet with his mother who had gone before them. Stefan loved music, dancing and playing his balalaika and wanted to perform, so as soon as he was older, he struck out on his own to Chicago. He performed at the Chicago Theater in Mischa's Balalaika Band. He was often sad and melancholy, which may have been because he missed his family and Russia, his homeland, though he never spoke of it. He had the fragile and sensitive nature of a musical artist.

The only thing the girls would hear Pa say about his old life was that he was "A White Russian" not a Red (Communist) Russian, and he claimed it loud and strong. He often drank too much beer, (Piwo pronounced peevo in Polish), and sometimes he would give one of the girls a nickel and we would go sneak him a bucket of beer from the tavern. A few times, he spent the night in the local jail where he sometimes was picked up for being drunk in public. He was a handsome man with piercing blue eyes, sandy blond hair and he was oh so talented. Everyone loved him, especially his daughters.

I once overheard this story from my corner in the dining room and I had to smile to myself just picturing it. "One day Ma heard gossip that a neighbor woman had set her sights on our Pa. She went hollering down the street after that woman waving a long Kielbasa sausage in the air at that woman in a threatening way telling her to stay away from her husband or else!" Yes, she was full of vim and vinegar, short little Ma and she had a temper when she needed it.

Ma loved to go see a movie with a quarter. Every so often, she would tell the girls to watch each other because she had to go to see the doctor and would sneak over to the movie theater. Her favorite was any movie with Nelson Eddy and Jeanette MacDonald and their romantic, glorious music. The movies with singing and dancing in them was a favorite of all of those Happel girls including Ma. Her final destination with or without her girls would be the

Hub or the Alvin Theater where she would sit in the dark and for a short time, blissfully disappear into a world so different than her own.

Ma loved her tall, handsome Russian balalaika player anyhow in spite of the fact he disappeared for weeks at a time for jobs. One thing about Ma, during all of the years we knew her, she never complained about anything and if she was hurting or sad, she always kept it to herself. In later years when she found out Pa was living with another woman, she never talked about it in front of the girls.

In Carrie's words shared with me one day, "When I met Stefan Habienko (Steve Happel), a most charming and talented man, I knew there was no one else for me. I first met him when I was working in a doctor clinic. He came in with a cut on his hand, and it took just a short time for me to give my heart to him forever."

But Carrie's love for him was not without a heavy cost. His life as a performer and musician was magical but also later became a burden on all of the family. One particularly difficult time in Carrie's life that the girls spoke of many years later was the saddest one of all. When Pa was absent from our home life more and more as we were getting older, Ma would never complain but would say that he was working rather than let us know he had moved in with another woman named Esther. One day, Esther came over to tell Ma that Pa was dying of cancer and that she would take good care of him and pay his hospital bills. All of us went with Ma to visit Pa at the state hospital for the last time, and shortly after that brief visit, we were told that he had died. We all got dressed up to go to his wake, and it was one of the saddest days of our lives. When we got to the funeral home, Esther came over to Ma at the door and told Ma that her parents and family did not know that our Pa had a wife and 6 daughters. She had but one request, that while we were there we could not tell anyone about that. One look at our Ma's hurt and sorrowful face as she nodded her head in acceptance, and we all finally agreed. So we had to quietly mourn our Pa as if we were mere shadows in his life, a secret. That was how Carrie Happel and her daughters said their last goodbye and quietly carried their memories and love for him forward with that heavy sadness in their hearts.

5

Understanding My Mother And Myself
Sunny's Story

I never wanted to be anything like my mother, Sunny. I am Kathleen Virginia Mary Veronica Weglarz and as a child, my long name given through Baptism, Confirmation, and my father's family name is as complicated and drawn out as my personality. It took many years, but one day I realized I am my mother and also my grandmother and probably those before her that I never even knew. I am proud, I am strong, I have a good sense of humor, I am loyal, I am capable, but that was not a confidence that came naturally. I have many flaws as well, but over the years, with much effort, I have tried to change the ones I could and accepted the ones I couldn't, while realizing that we all have shortcomings. It took a life full of challenges and pitfalls and eventually knowing my mother that I finally came to that realization about myself.

I remember many afternoons as I was growing

up, sitting at our kitchen table after school doing homework. I would start conversations with my mom, known to all as Sunny, while she was getting dinner ready. I was trying to avoid my homework as always. I was a captive audience while she prepared, cooked, or washed pots and dishes in the kitchen sink. I would start with "Mom, tell me about when you were growing up." It was easy to get her to share because we are a family of storytellers, and there were never many secrets. I can still hear her voice telling me "Sunny's Story" in her words and sharing so many little things about her life.

"Like everyone else growing up at that time in our neighborhood, we had very little money. One of my regular jobs when I was really young was to take a wagon and stand in line at the bakery for old bread or to the market with other little kids and wait for damaged or rotten fruit and vegetables.

"We got to be little beggars, but it didn't matter because food was scarce for all of us. If it couldn't be sold, we loaded it into our wagon and carted it home. We learned to haggle and be the first in line and act tough to get the food before the other kids or alternately, timid and sad to get the most from the grocery men. I got pretty good at acting," she would tell me.

"In the dirt alleys around our three flat, there

was all sorts of trash, and each week some of us kids would go trash picking with our wagon to see if there was anything we could use at home. One day when I was racing around the alley, I fell and hit my head on a rock. I ran crying back home to Alice, always the little mother, who yelled up to Ma on the third floor porch where she was hanging laundry. 'Sunny is bleeding all over, we need to take her to the doctor!'

Then Ma shouted down, 'We can't afford a doctor, use this bread!' And she threw down a loaf of bread. Alice pressed the pieces of bread against the cut, and eventually the bleeding slowed. When we went upstairs again, Ma hollered at us. 'You wasted a whole loaf of bread, no bread for supper now!'

"Every year at Christmas, the nice ladies at Erie Chapel would throw a big party with donated candy, cookies, and gaily wrapped presents under the big Christmas tree marked either for girl or boy. When Santa called your name, you could pick out one gift for yourself. One year, when I opened mine, I saw a beautiful big doll with blond curly hair. I had never had a doll before but had always wanted one. I was so happy! When I ran with it to show my mother, she took it home carefully and put it on the top shelf of the closet 'so it wouldn't get dirty or have your sisters break it,' she said. That was the last I ever saw of that doll. Ma sold it secretly for money to buy other things for the family.

"Erie Chapel was a little church a few blocks away that gave us clothing and food. When one of the children was considered sickly, the church paid to send that child away to a camp/school to be taken care of and fed until they gained weight and got healthier.

"Yep, you guessed it. I was the first girl in the family to be sent to Ridge Farm. I was sent there four times in my childhood. I was a skinny, lanky, pale little girl with allergies that seemed like a constant cold. I was so afraid of being taken away from my family. I was only around eight at the time when I was first sent away. I thought it would be like a prison for doing something wrong. Once I got there by train, carrying a little bag, they drove me with other girls that I didn't know to big dormitories with rows of beds. It was really far out in the country in Deerfield, Illinois. I had never gone anywhere alone and not farther than seven cents and a streetcar could take me so it felt like going to another state.

"All of the girls at Ridge Farm had clothes donated and warm coats because we were there for a school year, around seven months, and we got to go home at Christmas. We had a strict schedule; time to wake up, wash up, eat, and classes every day for around three hours.

"After dinner we told stories or read and then,

lights out early for sleep. Monday was Arithmetic; Tuesday was English and so on. Each day, we played outside and had nature classes, for fresh air. I always loved that time because we learned about different kinds of birds and animals that I had never seen before. We studied and grew flowers, my favorite subject. In our yard at home, there was only a tiny area of dirt with pieces of broken glass and rocks under the clotheslines next to the alley but sometimes a few weedy flowers would survive. So when I saw the beautiful fields of country flowers in spring, I was in heaven.

"Compared to my neighborhood at home, I eventually grew to love Ridge Farm more and after a time, I made friends and didn't want to go home. They had cats there and all of the girls played with them. That was when I found out that I was *really* allergic to cats.

"My eyes would start to water and my nose would run, and the nurses would say, 'That Sunny is the sickest little girl we have ever had. She can never get over her cold. We need to have her come back again.' So, I was sent back again and again. All I had to do is pet and play with the cats, and I knew I could be back again to Ridge Farm. They would send me back home for a couple of months in summer, and then I would be back to the Farm in fall for another session.

That lasted for about four years and then came the day they said I was getting too old to stay there again. My heart was broken.

"After a few years at Ridge Farm, it was getting much harder to go back home. I had to try to fit in again with my sisters, and I think they were jealous of me for getting to leave so often. Back at the Farm, I was taught good manners and things about nature and music, and these were things that just didn't fit into my other life with the family.

"At the farm, eventually I was known to be the most creative and dramatic and also kind of a leader. When we went ice-skating at the pond, the girls would always save the one pair of white ice skates for me. We were in little plays, and I was always the one who got picked for the main character. All of the younger girls loved to listen to me make up stories and games.

"Then, when I went home and finally got back to Motley School, I was a nobody, and it was hard to make new friends. I found out I was really behind in classes because I was away too long. I became quieter and more withdrawn.

"Even my sisters had new friends and didn't bother with me. It felt impossible to start over. My sister Alice helped me study, so I could finally graduate eighth grade, and I wore a borrowed white dress to the ceremony.

"When I was home, Erie Chapel and the children's choir was my happy place. I loved music more than anything. Though I never learned to read music, it was natural for me to sing in harmony. The music teacher, Miss Florence said I had a natural 'ear' for music. In those days, we all sang together for pastime, and my world was a happier place for that.

"When I was thirteen and just graduated from eighth grade, I helped to support the family. My older sisters and I were already serving tables at Juniors Hall with Ma when we could. Then, Ma got me my first job on my own as a maid and babysitter in Park Ridge. Ma put me on the train alone, once again, to the suburbs.

"When I arrived at a big house, I was given a room the size of a closet to sleep in with no light in it, just behind the kitchen. I had to do dishes, washing, cleaning, and serving. One day, my sister Alice came to visit me and when she saw the conditions I was living in and how hard I had to work, she made me pack up my few things and took me back home on the train.

"Once I got back home again, I had to bring in money for the family so I got assembly line jobs. One of them was at the Milky Way factory popping bubbles in the chocolate candy bars, the next was sewing thumbs on gloves, then lacing shoes at the Florsheim Shoe Company.

"I started moving up in the world when I became a waitress at the Chicago Athletic Club downtown. This job required me to carry a loaded big round tray of meals to each table. Problem was I was only about 90 pounds, and after a short time they let me go because they were afraid I would have an accident. I worked behind the candy counter at the movie theater and made lots of popcorn. I liked working at the movie theater.

"Finally, when I was 19, I proudly worked at Mrs. Stevens Chocolates, a specialty candy store in Downtown Chicago, and actually got to be an assistant manager there. I had a crisp white smock like a nurse with Mrs. Stevens embroidered on it. It was during the war, and sailors and soldiers would come in to get boxes of chocolates to send home to their sweethearts and mothers. Sometimes, they would try to make dates with me. I enjoyed flirting with those handsome young men, but I would never say yes.

"Almost everything I wore was a hand-me-down. In our neighborhood, there was a clothing store named Cinderella's. When I started working, all of my money went to Ma to help the family, but eventually, I was able to save a few quarters here and there for my own use, and I would go to Cinderella's and yearn for something just for me. I finally was able to put it on lay-away, so I paid a dollar down and a little each week until it was finally paid for. That is how I got my first brand-new pant suit.

"What I loved most at that time was ballroom dancing. My sisters, girlfriends, and I would go to dance halls where we could dance the night away to live bands. We would dance the polka, waltz, jitterbug and fox trot to our hearts content and practice our dance steps with each other when there were not enough boys around.

"One day, I saved enough money to go see Frank Sinatra, a new young singer we all swooned for. He was at the Chicago Theater in the loop, so I went with my girlfriend Ginny. We wanted to look more dressed up, so we took our worn out button front cardigan sweaters and turned the buttons around to the back. When we went to the ladies room and were in the stalls, we overheard a couple of catty girls say, 'Did you see those two dumb girls with their sweaters on backwards?' Then, they left the Ladies Room laughing. We waited with embarrassment, and then turned around our sweaters back to the front again.

"When I was a teenager, I used to go to Eckhart Park where all of the neighborhood kids would go for free fun. I used to hang around and started hearing some boys practicing their harmonicas in one of the rooms. I loved hearing them play and could just sit there for hours in a corner to listen. Jerry Murad was the head of the group and they called themselves the 'Harmonicats.'

"They eventually made some records, but they would practice there and I became their mascot. They gave me an autographed picture of themselves and I kept it for years and always loved their music, especially 'Peg 'O My Heart.'

"During those years, we saved up for a radio and would sit around it in the evenings and listen to scary stories like Inner Sanctum and turn off the light. The glow from the radio dial would mesmerize us. And, the frightening stories entertained us with sound effects so scary that we would cling together and let out an occasional shriek for which Ma would shush us.

"We liked soap operas and cried at some of the sad stories. It was so easy to sit and listen while gazing off at a distant point while painting an image in our minds of what the characters and surroundings would look like in this alternate world. We all giggled and laughed together at comedies like Burns and Allen.

"We listened to Don McNeill and *The Breakfast Club* every day, and one day went to see his show live at the Chicago Theater with Ma. Oh boy, were we shocked at what he really looked like! By his voice, we pictured him handsome and tall, but in person he was very short and very fat and his face was shiny with sweat. He was dressed in an ugly, baggy suit. After that, we didn't want to listen to his show again. It was then we all realized that what we heard on the radio was not real in the least, but only how we each would picture it in our vivid imaginations.

"I remember another day in 1939, when I was around fourteen years old and just starting to feel pretty confident about my little world. At that time, the citizens of Polish communities young and old were painfully aware of the horrible war that was moving across Europe. Each day, street corner newspaper boys would shout out the war headlines. 'Extra, Extra, read all about it!' Every night, families sat glued to the radio listening to the news of Poland. Ma still had relatives and friends there. Then the day came when the radio announcer broke into the music with the news that the German army had invaded Poland.

"We were listening to the Chicago Polish radio station, and they played the Polish national anthem and with great sorrow, they told us about the killing and suffering that was going on. We all gathered around Ma who was sitting at the kitchen table with her ear to the radio as she raised the volume up. She kept shaking her head in disbelief and had tears in her eyes.

"Reports were that the Nazis sent hundreds of bombers and by morning, whole sections of the city were destroyed. Men, women, and children were being killed and left in the streets, and there was nothing we could do to help. I had this horrible helpless feeling that gave me a stomach ache.

"Then again in 1941, just two years later on December 7th, the announcer on the radio shared more disastrous news that Japan had bombed Pearl Harbor, and so many American lives were lost.. Ma, who was always the strong one, had tears falling from her eyes. All of us girls gathered closely around each other as we listened to the reports together. At the end of that broadcast, they played God Bless America and we silently went to bed, huddled together with our sisters for comfort, each lost in our own thoughts.

"The stories of American sailors lost that horrible day kept repeating over and over on the radio. Newspaper hawkers at city corners again shouted out headlines to passers by. 'Extra, Extra, America at War!'

"That first Christmas Ma tried to celebrate. She cooked our favorite Polish dishes, but it was not about celebration but only a wish and prayer for peace. All of the songs about peace on earth and goodwill toward men that played in between the grim news of the war sounded so sad that year. Everyone walked around with a tired look in their eyes as we began to understand what was in store for us now that we were at war. Alice our eldest sister was married to Bill Markes by then and their first daughter, Karen, was born, Grandma's first grandchild. He joined the Army and was sent overseas, so our family already knew how hard those 'Goodbyes' were.

"Flags began to appear all over the neighborhood in front windows with a star for each son, father or husband in the military. As each blue star appeared, we said a prayer that it would not turn to a gold star, which meant that their son or husband was never coming back.

If you could ride a bike, you could get a job delivering telegrams. When people saw those boys riding down the street with a telegram, the neighbors would all silently stand by in concern because it was so often bad news that there was a war department notice of someone in their family was wounded, taken as a prisoner of war, or worse, killed in action. If they would come riding down our street, we would hold our breath in sorrow until the news was shared. If it passed your building you were safe, then you could breathe again.

"Life as we knew it was changing. Emotions were running high, so many boys from the neighborhood began to be seen in uniform. Every mother or father had mixed feelings of pride but also sadness and fear as their sons went overseas. All of the latest neighborhood gossip was about whose son or brother was going to be a soldier or sailor and worse, reports of those not coming home.

"At the train stations, sometimes soldiers would give out pieces of paper to girls with their name and camp address written on them hoping they would get a girl to write to them. Some girls did and many loyally kept in touch with their soldiers often until their mail became 'Sealed With a Kiss.'

"The kids in the neighborhood took wagons to collect scrap metal and rubber for the war effort. Ration stamps became a daily food problem, and Victory Gardens became essential to turn even the stingiest plot of earth into a place to grow some fresh vegetables, and we tried our best. Blackouts in many cities became mandatory in fear of bombing, and Chicago was no exception. Some of us were afraid because there wasn't any real shelter to provide any protection between the bombs and us. During those times, we were in a second or third floor apartment, unprotected. In our childish imagination, a bomb could easily have hit our building and killed many of us and we were afraid, even though our plucky, brave Ma said that wouldn't happen.

"Every Sunday our President Roosevelt broadcast his fireside chat to let us know how Americans were working hard toward victory and how everyone was doing his or her part and should feel proud. During those war years, we went to see movies at the show more often and waited, eyes glued to the screen for the newsreels to see what was going on in the war. During those war years, some nights, we walked to the corner tavern where we danced and sang to the jukebox full of all our favorite songs. We would all raise a glass and toast the boys who were shipping out and sing together that heartfelt song 'I'll Be Seeing You' about all the old familiar places of our old neighborhood. Then, we would dance the Jitterbug to get 'In The Mood' with Glenn Miller. The Andrews Sisters' quirky rendition of 'Boogie Woogie Bugle Boy,' was a always a big favorite, but the Andrews Sisters had nothing to show better than the Happel Sisters. We could dance and sing with the best of them and we even curled our hair-do's like them. The saddest of all the wartime songs was 'I'll Be Home For Christmas' which brought tears to our eyes because the war raged on for way too long and many a Christmas was so difficult for all of our lonely soldiers and their loving families waiting back home.

"At the beginning of the war, I was sitting with my sisters on the front steps as all the neighbors would do toward the end of each day. Walking down the street came a handsome soldier in his uniform. He asked us, 'Is this where Carrie Happel lives?' I said, 'Yes, that's my Mother.' And the younger girls eagerly said, 'Come on, we can take you up there.' They proceeded to run up the stairs with a clatter as he followed. They shouted, 'Ma, someone's here to see you.' When Ma took one look at him, she cried out. 'Oh, my God!' and with tears in her eyes, hugged him to her heart. We girls gathered around while Ma introduced him, 'This is your brother, George.'

"We all stood there with our mouths wide open in shock! She had never told us about the life she had before us and we were in awe of this tall, good-looking stranger. Ma had not seen him since a very young age.

"That day, he came to visit Ma before he shipped out to places unknown, and we wrote to him during the war. After the war, he came to visit us when he could. We found out in that most unexpected way that Ma was married to Julian Kuscynski before our dad and had three sons with him. She went to be his housekeeper at the age of 13, then married him a short time later.

"Together they had three sons by the time she was 22 when the third baby boy, George, was born. Ma left all of them and moved to another part of the city to stay with her husband's sister until they divorced. As far as we knew, she never visited with the boys again until that day George came to surprise her. So, that's how the Happel sisters came to meet their half-brother George and learn about their mother's mystery.

"It is so hard to even imagine her leaving her three sons so many years before, especially with one only three years old.

"We never learned what heartache and misery she must have suffered or why she chose to leave. That would have crushed any other mother and yet she never complained.

Carrie's youngest son was George Kusczynski. After he left the service, he changed his name legally, moving to Bakersfield, CA; He married and become manager of the Padre Hotel. He stayed in touch with Ma and us, his half sisters, until he passed away many years later. As far as we knew, none of Carrie's other sons were ever in touch with her again.

As a young girl, hearing these stories from my mother and her sisters, I had many moments just wondering how Grandma Carrie had made it through so many sad valleys of her life. According to Carrie's daughters, there were never any terrible temper tantrums, or highly emotional dramatics. She kept her thoughts and fears to herself.

Keeping her secrets locked safely in her heart, while knowing she could never go back must have been unbearable, but yet she continued steadfastly on her difficult path.

"One day when Ma and Nancy were just walking out of the Alvin Theater after seeing a movie, everyone on the street was yelling and cheering and shouting 'The war is over!' People were coming out into the street from all over and dancing and hugging with joy and relief. There were also many tears added to the mix of emotions as prayers of thanks crossed the lips of so many war-weary people."

6

The Story Of Sunny And Casey
Notes on Relationships and Romance

My mom Sunny had a carved wooden bible
box, about the size of a cigar box, that held her
collection of "treasured" things. Over the years, she
was prone to cleaning it out, whenever she wasn't
having a happy time. If there was something in the box
that held a memory tinged with sadness or frustration,
out it went into the trash. As a result, Mom had very
few personal things left in that box by the time she
passed away at 86. It was simple for my sister and I to
easily divide her few remaining treasures between us.

In the box was her birth certificate yellowed
with age and cracking at the edges. A tiny gold cross
on a chain my dad gave to her while she waited for
him during the war and a gold ankle bracelet with a W
engraved in the middle and on 4 hearts, one in each
corner, each of our initials; S, C, K and J for Sunny,
Casey, Kathy and Janice. There was a collection of
funeral holy cards from Daddy's death, the death of his

parents and of her mother, and some cards of her precious sisters that she missed so much. The box also contained her marriage license and a couple of fragile much-creased letters from my father, Casey, from when he was in the Army. When I later looked through her things, I recognized his handwriting and smiled just thinking about what a rascal he was.

My mom, Sunny, used to tell me the story that she had not one, but two men who wanted to marry her. "Eddie had money," she said. "He would have given me anything that I wanted, and he even offered me a diamond ring."

In those days, that was no small thing. Especially coming from the level of poverty that she and her sisters were raised in. But according to her, "I just couldn't get Casey out of my mind. He had just joined the Army, but I still picked him. Casey was around six feet tall and had a charming grin that he used so well. All the girls and even my sisters liked him. He was a brown haired, brown eyed, lanky, gum chewing, Casanova and oh, so handsome in his uniform. In those days I was pretty cute, too." She recalled. Casey called me his "Blond Bombshell."

"We girls had no nylons due to war rationing, so we used to draw a line down the back of each calf to look like seamed nylons, which were the fashion. We always hoped it wouldn't rain and smear it. I used

Coty loose face powder with a powder puff and Maybelline mascara in a little sliding red box that we would open, spit on a little brush and rub it into the black stuff and put it on our eyelashes before it dried.

"If we dared to cry, it would smear and run down under our eyes. What a mess that could be! So, back to your father. In those days, he never bought me little gifts like Eddy did because his family was poor like us. One day, when we were first dating, he did bring me a little gift in a crumpled brown paper bag. It was a pound of dark red cherries from the fruit market but half of them were eaten already. I knew what a pound of cherries feels like! My mom and sisters quickly left the room and I remember them giggling in the kitchen making fun and calling him cheap. Anyways, I turned Eddie down, and wrote to my Casey.

"At that time one of my favorite songs was 'Dream,' and when I was feeling blue, I would hear this song and sing the melody to myself knowing my life was not as bad as I sometimes felt it was. Oh boy, I was such a dreamer. I was 19 years old in 1944, and I imagined that one day I would get married and hoped and prayed that Casey would be the one who would pick me.

"He wrote only a couple of letters to me, and when the first one came, he didn't even remember my last name. But he got the address right, and luckily, there was only one Evelyn on my block. He didn't even remember that everyone called me Sunny. I was so happy anyways! He wasn't much of a writer and sent a short postcard every so often. Whenever he came home on leave, I went with him to the neighborhood bar where everyone knew his name, of course. When I first met him, I was flirting with him and asked, 'How do you like this new lipstick?' He looked at me with that cute, crooked grin while moving in toward my face, looking closely at my lips, he answered, 'I can't tell, can I taste it?' (Here in her story, she would get all fluttery) You see, he wanted to give me a little kiss, so I said 'Sure,' and I opened the Max Factor tube of Rocket Red, swiveled it up and handed it to him and walked away. We were always teasing like that our whole life together.

"We loved to dance and have a few beers at the tavern and he was always such fun to be with, but I wanted him for myself. He was a loud, funny, friendly sort of guy and loved spending time with his darn buddies. After boot camp, when he was getting ready to take a train back to Greensborough, North Carolina he gave me a gold chain with a little gold cross and asked me to wait for him till he got back. And I did.

"One day almost a year later, I got an unexpected visit from Casey. His Mom died suddenly after surgery and he was on leave for her funeral. My sisters, Ma, and I all went to the wake. Six months later, his father Josef died suddenly, and Casey was home again with an Honorable Discharge. Plans for our wedding by next July became the logical thing for us to do. I was so excited to be getting married, but Casey wanted to get married in a Catholic Church.

"First, I had to take catechism classes and sign a paper that I would raise my children Catholic. I hated that I felt forced, because I loved the friendly, generous people at Erie Chapel, they were always there for my family, but I went along with his wishes. Casimir Edward Weglarz, soon to be my husband, was raised Catholic by his parents. They came to America from Poland and strived to be hard-working good Americans. All three of their children went to Holy Innocents Catholic School, and even though they had little money, they paid what they could for tuition. It was really important for their children to get the best education, and they gave up much to make that happen. Casey remembered the nuns and priests with much respect as he was taught to do, so in order to become his wife, I promised that I would do that too.

"I had no money for a wedding dress and really wanted to have something special for that day. Casey saved his white silk parachute from his Army Air Force days, and so I had a dress made out of it.

"July 6, 1946 was our wedding day, and from that day forward, I moved in to his parents flat to help take care of Joe and Irene and their big cat Oscar who ruled the household. I was terrified of Oscar, and he did everything he could to make me miserable including making me sneeze constantly. He was the family cat and they loved him. Ahhh choooo!"

So, from here I'll continue the story of my parents, Sunny and Casey, that I learned about over the years. Their lives together went forward as the sands of time continued to trickle to the bottom of the hourglass. After a few years, Sunny and Casey started their lives over on their own, finally just the two of them. Casey worked two jobs, and Sunny kept house and experimented with cooking, ruining most recipes.

Casey always loved baseball and was on a softball league, so Sunny went to watch him play ball. When she used to sit in the stands, sometimes she would overhear other fans comment on what a loud mouth and bad temper that guy at first base had.

That guy was her husband Casey, but she wisely kept it to herself. There wasn't an umpire who took kindly to his constant commentary from first base. "Throw da bum out!" and other various comments peppered every game. Casey was a colorful fella, indeed. Together, they went to meet friends at the corner tavern and continued to tease and bicker with each other as the years went by.

They were always trying to make their marriage work. When Sunny tried to teach Casey how to do a polka, no matter how they tried, when she went up, he went down. When she stepped right, he stepped left. Their relationship was always the same as that dance. Though the music was familiar and enjoyed, they were never really in step with each other. They never stopped *trying* to stay in step with each other throughout their lives and that was surely a sign of true love.

For Sunny and Casey, the birth of their two daughters was a miracle. They didn't expect just how much responsibility the new role of Mommy and Daddy was going to be. It was in the years right after the war and everyone was starting to rebuild their lives so we were a result of the "Baby Boom." When my sister Janice and I were just babies, they bought a candy store on the corner of George and Hamlin Street. They had never owned a business before, so they learned everything together. The four of us lived in a tiny, dingy apartment at the back of the store, complete with cockroaches and other critters, much to the dismay of my mother. Janice and I spent most of our time either behind one of the candy counters, hiding in one of the booths, sitting at the soda fountain stools, or hanging from Mom's hip as she worked around the store with Dad, seven days a week. There was a neon lighted jukebox always playing top 10 hits, and that was when my own love of music began. The neighborhood people that came in regularly became our extended family.

After a couple of years of hard work and long hours, they decided it was no way to raise a family, so they put a new plan into action. Dad got a job at the Manufacturers National Bank in the city, and they sold the Candy Store. They bought the little house on Argyle Street for $13,000.00 with a hefty G.I. mortgage and that became our haven from that day forward.

Mom and Dad loved my sister and I unconditionally, but occasionally they would have bitter arguments, especially after parties when they had a few too many drinks. Janice and I remembered a number of times they would wake us from our sleep with arguing, punctuated with crashing sounds of things thrown for effect. During one post party episode, in a surge of anger, Mom dared Daddy to set fire to the house, then he started piling up newspapers in the center of the living room floor along with things he could burn. Mom called her friend Pat from across the street who came and got us to stay at their house.

All I could think of was to grab the birdcage and save my parakeets Nippy and Peppy. It was

December and it was cold and snowy, so Pat Ramion got my sister and I bundled in coats over our PJ's and hurried us across the street to her house with a bath towel over the birdcage to keep the birds warm. Needless to say, there was no fire and we were returned to a quiet house about an hour later, that battle over and done with. Another time, Mom took my sister and I to stay with her sister Alice in the city. We took the bus carrying shopping bags with our clothes and underwear, thinking that Mom would leave Daddy forever. Thankfully, as things always ended, we went back home to him after one day. The fierce arguments, making up, and starting over was a pattern we were used to but the fear remembered in our little hearts lingered for many years.

Before closing the lid on Mom's box of treasured things from her life, I lovingly replaced her familiar small collection of lace-bordered hankies that her Ma gave to her over the years.

There was the delicate one that I remembered with a hot pink crochet lace trim that exactly matched the gown she wore the day of my wedding. When she tucked it into her little purse that day, she had a soft smile on her lips, probably thinking of her mother Carrie who could not be there for our special day. A familiar bit of cherished memory that was again passed along with Grandma's love. Do we ever realize how many gifts we are given while we're growing up? Not the much awaited store bought gifts, but the gifts that return to us during a lifetime in little bits and pieces. The little permanent scenes in our minds like a vintage film that flickers through our memories. Those are the most precious gifts of all.

7

In Retrospect

Lessons I learned from Mom

My mother Sunny was a woman of many personalities. Just when we would think we knew her, she would surprise us with another side of her personality. Her moods ranged from funny to sad, insecure to confident, angry to loving, fearful to brave, reverent to irreverent. She loved to tell all kinds of jokes (and occasionally a good dirty joke, much to our embarrassment) and would print copies of them to share. We would seldom see her cry, but she was very sentimental especially listening to her music. She thrived in the company of family and friends, and she loved parties and games. She would watch game shows on TV and spend hours writing out dozens of cards with party questions, so she could use them to entertain everyone. She would listen to song lyrics and write them out on sheets for us to sing when we got a group together. When Dad got a copy machine at work, she was ecstatic to send with him her hand written creations to make copies of to pass out and share. In winter, when we were growing up, she would put on her winter coat on and tie her babushka—A babushka is a Russian/Polish word for a headscarf, which is the style all women from the old neighborhood wore in winter to keep their heads warm—around her head and dress my sister and me in layers of warm clothes, then get us outside for any fresh air activities she could think up.

She taught us how to create snow forts and invited the neighborhood kids over to help. Once, she tried to make an ice skating pond in the backyard and spent a whole day freezing pair after pair of gloves in that hopeless attempt while muttering under her breath words my sister and I were not supposed to hear. That one made her really mad because she liked to have her way and Mother Nature was not going to cooperate with her.

When there were tornado warnings and that wailing neighborhood siren came on, she would panic and send my sister and me into the coat closet to sit on the floor in the musty dark while she kept watch, "just in case."

Mom was definitely not the type of mother that was popular on TV during that era. They presented meals to their families wearing pearls and a housedress with an apron over it while serving creative dishes every meal. She didn't like to cook and had her few traditional recipes that rotated on a regular schedule. Somehow, she was always busy at the stove making something for dinner. She didn't like spices and sauces and adapted recipes to what she called "American style."

Mom never was drawn into new fad recipes or anything "foreign or exotic" that some housewives became addicted to at that time. She hated new foods. She didn't trust them.

A can of Campbell's soup heated up with a slice of bread and butter or a hot dog was her idea of a good meal. She tried to get us to eat fried bologna and onions, or liver and onions, but we would have no part of it, so she would eat those herself relishing their flavor and make us something else.

Our mother was the opposite of the motto "Variety is the spice of life," and we had no choice in the matter. Her basic meal list consisted of any of these foods. In the meat group category there was plain baked chicken breasts in the oven, a beef rump roast sliced and simmered on top of the stove in gravy for hours—sometimes tender, sometimes not, American chili, American spaghetti, American Chop Suey, plain meatloaf with no spices and no seasonings. But, occasionally as a special treat, there was a smoked polish sausage for Dad who missed Polish food.

In the vegetable food group there was baked potatoes—she was allergic to potatoes, so no mashed, fried or any other kind, canned corn, or peas rounded out our menus, and sometimes there was a salad with a few cut tomatoes mixed with iceberg lettuce and always topped with Wishbone Thousand Island dressing.

Friday was meat-less in a Catholic family, so usually we had stinky tuna sandwiches on squishy soft white Wonder Bread. It also might be egg salad sandwiches or canned Campbell tomato soup with a whole pack of saltine crackers crumbled on top. A can of Tuna mixed with a can of cream of mushroom soup with a can of peas mixed in, was a wild card at meals, served over a piece of toast. I need not say more on that subject.

A Betty Crocker she was not, but we always had a meal on the table. She and dad grew up with little food during the depression and during the rationing of the war years, so they felt that we had an abundance of good food and were grateful for it.

If we didn't eat what was put on our plate, Daddy would insist in a booming voice that could scare the feathers off a bird. We couldn't leave the table unless we ate it, but most times Mom would intervene, and we would finally be given the OK to leave the table. It seemed to my sister and me that

Mom didn't eat much or like food very much, it was never a priority to her but she provided for us the best she knew how.

When the first McDonalds opened on Harlem Avenue, it took weeks and lots of pleading with Mom and Dad to take us to try it. It was the first fast food we had ever tasted, and of course we loved it. That became the Saturday night treat for the family for many years.

When TV Dinners came on the market, Mom was thrilled! Then, many nights we would have a choice of Salisbury steak or Turkey with dressing. She always washed and saved those crinkly tins in case she could use them for some kind of craft project.

Of all the food groups, her favorite was dessert. Sweets from the bakery would put a sparkle in her eyes, especially cream filled coffee cake. Once or twice a year, she baked Icebox cookies or Oatmeal cookies—all of her cookies were small and crunchy, mostly good for dunking in milk or coffee.

Toffee squares with melted Hershey Chocolate were her favorite, and her specialty in summer was a big pan of apple slices with a sugar drizzle. The apples were picked from our trees. In our family, Saturday was a Deli day, she sent Dad to Harczack's a Polish Deli for fresh sliced lunchmeat (Polish Ham or Salami), bakery rolls, fresh baked rye bread and

Kolachki's, made of tender dough, covered with powdered sugar and filled with apricot jam as a treat for us.

Mom was a stay at home mother, and during those post war years that was a pretty common thing. She eventually would get bored and think we needed to bring in extra money, with our help of course. She worked her way up.

First ordering boxes of screws and bolts in heavy boxes. Janice, Mom and I would sit at the table and twist the bolts onto the screws then she would mail the whole heavy batch back. Then there was Avon calling, we helped pack orders and deliver catalogs. That was fun for all of us, testing the samples and scents with Here's My Heart and Topaz fragrances filling our rooms. After that there were Tupperware parties and learning how to burp the tops. Boring for us, but Mom got a whole cabinet full of Tupperware that she kept using until they became gummy with wear after way too many years.

Finally, she got a part time job at Turnstyle in the silk flower department for a couple of afternoons a week. After two days, she quit because she wanted to be her own boss. She stewed for a while following that job, and one day a total surprise met my sister and I when we came home from school.

I was a sophomore in high school and when I

came home one day and found the living room filled
with boxes. Janice and I looked at the boxes in awe
and I called out to Mom in the other room, "Mom,
what's all this?" She came in acting like it was an
everyday occurrence. She told us she had been to the
Chicago Merchandise Mart and decided to open a
shop. We were stunned and when I asked her if she
knew how to do that? She said she would figure it out
as she went along. My poor dad came home and was
just as perplexed as we were, but she reassured us all
that she had big ideas already. She sure did, because in
one week, she found a storefront in the neighborhood,
signed the contract and started to clean, paint and put
dad to work building shelves and putting up peg-board
for displays. That was the beginning of Sunny's Gift
Shop. Her sign was hung and we became a business
owning family once again. We all chipped in working
there dividing up the shifts because Sunny's was open
seven days a week. Janice, her dearest friend Judy and
I filled in when Dad was working his day job at the
bank. Because of Mom, it became a success, so she
opened a second store in nearby area, but a short time
after that she sold them both and made a tidy little
profit.

    After my sister and I were out of high school
and she had sold her gift shops, Mom got a job at
Aberdeen's Florist. She always loved flowers and

arranging and had a natural talent. Unfortunately, she was still allergic to some kinds of flowers, but she stuck it out with her runny nose and red eyes and was on the way to being a designer.

The big news was when she helped create the wedding flowers for Tiny Tim's wedding. He was a strange ukulele playing celebrity and his marriage to Miss Vickie made front-page news, and Aberdeen's was his choice of florist. She worked there just long enough to buy wholesale and to learn to make all of our wedding bouquets and flowers arrangements when Janice and I got married, and that was a lovely offering with a creative personal touch from her.

All of her years, she challenged herself from one accomplishment to another. She was self-taught at everything. One day, she saw an old baby grand piano at a garage sale and begged my dad to buy it. When it filled up the space in the den, she taught herself how to play by picking out tunes by ear. After that was gone, she bought an organ and sat in the living room fiddling with all of the different sound effect knobs until she began to play the popular tunes she so loved. Lara's theme from Dr. Zhivago was her favorite, and we must have heard it in different variations at least four hundred times in our lifetime.

Mom began painting with acrylic paints and had daddy frame them. She had sales in her home and at the church bazaar each year with all of her art pieces. She badgered dad to go into the old neighborhood to Maxwell Street to find bargains and claimed somebody's trash can become someone else's treasure.

She and dad worked at helping some pretty ugly pieces find rebirth again, whether from their weekly garage sales and estate sale hunting or going to Maxwell Street. Even when my sister and I got married, she would bring over to us some of her treasures and take us to the hot spots and teach us how to bargain. For me, that was the beginning of my lifelong love of antiques and vintage treasure finds. When country crafts began to be popular, she talked daddy into going to the senior center in the neighborhood and cut out wood shapes, and then she turned them into rustic pieces of home décor after she painted and crafted them.

She was a very dramatic but loving mother, and I can attest that life was never boring growing up, nor was it easy for me. Sometimes she would get moody and lash out in intense anger that no one wanted to mess with.

Being the eldest daughter, I tried to remain as independent from her as soon as I was able and I think that hurt her feelings, though she never said anything. Because of that, I was always battling my feelings of guilt, for I loved her but hated her sadness. I just couldn't bear the burden of feeling responsible for her happiness, and I felt a coward in that respect. I learned so many lessons both good and bad from her.

She seemed prone to depression especially in winter when she was cooped up and also had emotional mood swings that were unpredictable. Sometimes, she had a volatile temper. To compensate for that, she never stopped trying to make things better again. She never gave up on anything or on her family. If something disappointed her, she would just keep chipping away until the situation became manageable.

Mom didn't like the dark and when Dad died, after we had moved to California, she had a very hard time living alone. My sister Janice made many a trip into the city to spend time with her, until she sold the house on Argyle and moved to Windsor Park Manor for active adults (senior citizens) in Carol Stream, closer to my sister. That surely was a beautiful, elegant place to live, and her little studio was just fine with her. They had a lovely formal dining room in a building that looked like an English Manor House and a full cooking staff to prepare and serve meals, and she really enjoyed that. I don't think she ever cooked again in her little kitchenette, and she gave away all of her pots, pans and dishes, keeping only one or two pieces from her old kitchen when she moved in. While living there at Windsor Park, she had two boyfriends that she played pool with, had card games and watched TV together with. She always kept arms distance from them with a twinkle in her eye and never forgot her Casey.

In her later years, she became more easy-going and grew more contented and more settled. She tried her hand at writing some songs and a little poetry and was so proud of her accomplishments. Mom loved self-help sayings, and that was another treasure trove of copies she shared with everyone. I used to laugh when she would give me another copy, reading some out loud as if to impress me with their importance. Surprisingly in my later years, I began to take them to heart. Here are a few examples of the many sayings she kept, and she would take her copies out again from time to time to inspire herself:

"The secret to a happy life is to only dread one day at a time."

"Don't replace one worry with another."

"Life is never picture perfect."

"People make mistakes and sometimes, bad choices. But it's what you learn from those experiences that make all the difference."

My mother shared with me after my dad had passed away, that she never pictured herself being alone even for a day without my father, her Casey being by her side. She said she was always trying to mold him into a perfect friend and husband. She was always fighting to fill the voids in herself that she was never able to fill.

She said she felt abandoned by her father and wanted Casey to always be there for her. She didn't like to share him with other people. She enjoyed activities and always wanted Casey to share them with her even if he didn't enjoy them. She said she was afraid of being alone after being sent to Ridge Farm and away to jobs by herself. She wanted her husband to take care of her and pamper her and share her interests. He never understood that about her and strained against those reins their whole married life, and that resulted in many arguments between them. Their bickering was notorious.

One morning, after another breakfast "pep talk" on how they could get along better, she found him dead of a massive heart attack in another room after she got off the phone with her friend. The light in her life was forever dimmed from that moment forward. She said she realized too late that she had too many expectations of him. I had never heard her whisper this phrase before with tears in her eyes and never would hear it again, "I was so wrong." She carried with her so many regrets that haunted her the rest of her days, only wishing to have a chance to do it over again.

Getting to know my mother was something of a challenge over a period of many years. Even after she was gone, I thought of her so often and a flashback would lead to an *Ah ha* moment where I would suddenly seem to understand her more.

The ever-changing kaleidoscope that was my mother didn't become clear to me until many years later, after my children were grown up and had children of their own. I was finally able to thoughtfully look back trying to make sense of my own life. I can see mannerisms in myself that were hers and ideas and interests pop into my head that I dream up to occupy myself as she did.

Now that I'm old, my hair has turned to white, and my body is slowly changing and doesn't work as well as it used to, I've realized just how much I have become my mother over the years and that's not such a bad thing. It's finally as comfortable as my old slippers.

8

Kathy's Story: My Childhood
The Early Years: The House On Argyle Street

Before my mother Sunny passed away in her eighties, on one of my visits home from California, my sister Janice and I took Mom to our old neighborhood. We wanted to see again the neighborhood that Janice and I grew up in. As we got out of the car to look around, we each were lost in our memories of that house so full of life, tears and of laughter. Our old house had been torn down, and a narrow three-story duplex was squeezed in on the lot, bare of the apple orchard with familiar trees and bushes. Now, the streets and houses that I had once known as well as the back of my hand had all changed. There were strangers now living in the houses lining the streets. The beloved people, who had been our extended family all those years ago, had either moved away as we did, or passed away. Those same streets seemed twenty feet wider 50 years ago and, surprisingly, now looked like little roads and the homes seemed much smaller. Our eyes prickled with tears of loss.

How could anyone know, when living through their childhood that they would someday look back with longing? That those years would be the good old days? No one tells us, "This is the happiest you will ever be in your life." That time, that place, that feeling. What would I give to find that feeling, that moment, again for a day or even an hour? It's as impossible as trying to catch smoke in your hand. The thing I miss most in the world is gone forever. If only I could go back to my childhood, walk down the hall to my room, climb into my old bed, and wake up seeing my whole future laid out before me like a red carpet so I could pick the direction of my happiness, choose all of my favorites like candy from a candy counter or the best chapters of a well read book.

I will cradle the little house on Argyle Street in my heart, always. Across the decades, as I remember looking out the front picture window, I can look back at my first memories. Even as a little girl, my brain rejected the idea of forgetting anything. I know now as I age, my memories are starting to fade into pastel colors, not as vivid as they once were long ago. Not lost yet, but I feel the urgency of putting these memories to paper.

My memory of moving to our house on Argyle Street is still crystal clear. In the beginning, our house was at the end of a dirt and gravel road across from the Big Oaks Golf Course. There were massive old oak trees along the road. No paved streets, no streetlights, no sidewalks, and our mailbox was at the next corner on a wooden post for us to walk to each day to pick up mail. Sunny and Casey had to have that little dream house for their own and took out a mortgage, which was a scary thing in those days.

The year that I was six and Janice was three, on a warm and sunny spring day, we finally saw our house out the car window for the first time as mom pulled up in the old Buick. We were all packed into the car with Auntie Florence and our cousins Sandy and Larry who were the same ages as we were. They squeezed a kid sized table and four little chairs in the trunk with cherry Kool-aid and cookies. The four of us kids stared in awe at the whole green lawn full of sunny yellow dandelions in full bloom. Although they were weeds, they were so beautiful to us for we had never seen anything like that in the city. This vivid carpet of flowers spread out before us over the whole lawn. We spent the day picking them and getting our fingers sticky and noses yellow with pollen from pressing the flowers to our little faces to smell. I didn't realize then that we were so envied, because my parents were the first of the family to move from inner city flats to what was then considered "a house in the country." We followed the big bumblebees over lots of clover blooming sweetly in the lawn. We would sit and pick wild violets for hours then learned later to make little bouquets or wreaths for our hair. The tiny ranch house on more than an acre of land with fruit trees and flowers was a little gem of a home.

6814 Argyle Street was an address that meant a lot to many people for many years. I have never been one to remember numbers. In fact, I have always been numerically deficient. In other words, anything with numbers has always swirled in my mind in confusion, never settling in their proper place. That address stuck permanently in my memory, and I always remembered our phone number.

We had a yellow wall phone with a big rotary dial on the wall of the utility room with a cord that stretched for yards. It was a busy phone line for my mom had no other connection to her sisters, and she missed them terribly when we first moved. It began as a shared party line where if you wanted to call out, there may be another neighbor talking on the line.

Respectfully, a quick sorry and hang up, was our only alternative and try again in a few minutes. When the phone company expanded our neighborhood lines we got to keep our first and only phone number Spring-4-2282 all by ourselves and that was quite a luxury.

Mom was the workhorse doing cleaning, cooking, laundry and yard work all year long. The house had dark brown tile floors throughout, only two bedrooms, one bathroom, and a tiny kitchen for the four of us to live in. It was, at the time, just big enough. The yard was a paradise to my sister and me! Grape vines and raspberry bushes, apple trees, plum trees, and cherry trees thrived in abundance.

My poor city mom didn't know what to think of it all. She was used to spending time with her sisters in the city and they didn't drive, so visiting them was going to be a rare treat for her. Dad worked at Manufacturers National Bank on Ashland Avenue in the "old neighborhood."

From the time Mom and Dad moved to the house on Argyle Street that's what they called it when they would go into the city. "Let's go to the old neighborhood this weekend" would bring a smile to Mom's lips as she waited for those days.

"Thoughts on the subject of jeans"...Ha, got your attention! I meant genes. Before I go any further, I couldn't give credence to my memoir unless I shared some of my thoughts on this subject. What a miracle life is in relation to how each of us are made up of a mix of the genes we inherit from our parents and those before them. It's a pretty heavy subject but so

important.

In trying to piece together the history of my family and connect the dots to create a picture, you can see that I am most moved by the strength of the women who preceded me. In all fairness, I have inherited genes from not only the Happel side of the family but also the Weglarz branch of the family tree.

Even though I'm a hopeless romantic, picturing "the good ol' Days," I'm also painfully aware that those were extremely hard times for women. It was especially tough for those immigrants coming from other countries in that era.

My Father's mother, Mary Rzesikowska was born in Poland and immigrated to the United States in 1907 at the age of fourteen. After she married Jan Weglarz in Chicago, her first child died just after birth but then they were blessed with three more children. I never got to know her because she passed away before I was born, but I can see that I have inherited many of her physical characteristics because I have photographs of her and I see them repeated in my Aunt Irene and my cousin Jacqueline who are the only females from that ancestral line. We have similar body shapes and features, same smiles and eyes.

When I hear them speak, even our voices have the same tone, and it always surprises me because it's like listening to myself speak when I hear them talking.

It makes me smile, because I think my Grandmother Mary must have sounded like us, too. I learned about her in later years through my Auntie Irene.

She shared with me that her mother was a very ladylike woman and had beautiful manners. Even though they had very little money, Mary would still keep her home pretty and clean. She would invite her lady friends over for "tea" and used her nice dishes. She had a sweet, gentle nature, a great sense of humor, and rarely complained about anything. In her way, she raised her children by her example that courtesy is owed, respect is earned and love is given, and they thrived in her teachings. Mary Weglarz was a very devout woman who loved her family more than anything on earth. Sadly, my grandmother Mary passed away suddenly at the tender age of forty-five after a complicated surgery, leaving behind her husband Jan who died six months later of "a broken heart."

At the time, her eldest son, my father Casey, was in the army. Casey was twenty-two and was given an honorable discharge to return home and raise his brother and sister, Joe age seventeen, and Irene only thirteen. I have always felt that there was something missing from our lives to be robbed of her life when she was so young. My father was so heartbroken to lose his mother when she died that he was never able to speak of her, but then, he always held his emotions very close to his heart. It would be my honor to think that I inherited some of the strong genes from this special lady, and I would hope and pray that she would be proud of me.

"Our bank"...Daddy worked at the Manufacturer's National Bank for 45 years starting work as a teller and eventually moving up to Assistant Vice-President. He spoke Polish fluently, and that bank was in the center of a neighborhood that had the largest concentration of Polish immigrants living in the United States besides Warsaw, Poland.

Everyone loved Casey! Each day Dad would drive our one car to the city and be home at dinnertime. If Mom needed the car for something or the weather was particularly freezing or snowy, Dad would leave the car for her and he would walk to the bus stop a few blocks away. Taking the bus into the city for work could take him up to an hour or more each way. For many years he worked an additional job later in the day at a currency exchange to bring in extra money. He was always hard working and never complained about being tired or stressed. He had to pay the bills, but his family was always his priority and his house was his little kingdom, so he made it clear to us it was all worth it to him.

When my sister and I were both babies, Mom would take us on the bus into the city to visit him at the bank. We girls felt like we owned that amazing building. We were in awe whenever we entered the bank, that gothic cathedral of marble and gold with a ceiling as high as the sky.

She would slide us over his marble counter and under the heavy bulletproof glass to visit him behind the scenes. He never cared if it broke any rules because when his girls came, we where his princesses. He would take us on a tour every time saying hello to all the other workers and open the vault doors showing us stacks of money on carts. We never get tired of that.

"Daddy and "the silver service"... Every year the bank had a year-end appreciation banquet at the downtown Conrad Hilton Hotel. Mom always hated that he would be gone until so late and would get anxious each time. As usual, he would have a few too many drinks with the guys and when Mom greeted him at the door, he would present to her a nice piece of solid silver serving ware or a complete place setting of silverware that he had filched from the table when no one was looking. She was appalled and told him if he kept that up, one day he was going to be caught. Oh,

the embarrassment of it all in her eyes.

The first time it was a sugar bowl, then a coffee server followed by salt and pepper shakers, then a nice little tray. One year, he came home with a large creamer, and his suit coat and shirt were heavily soaked with cream. He said he kept his eye on it all night until it was empty, but someone must have refilled it when he wasn't looking before he quickly stuck it under his suit coat to head home. After ruining a perfectly good Sears Roebuck and Co. suit, he decided that was the last piece he would ever bring home. I guess he learned his lesson, and we got a good laugh over it. No more ever needed to be said.

"Grocery days"... Mom, Janice, and I walked almost a mile each way to the National grocery store in the neighborhood. It was the only store when we first moved there. It could be drizzly, or cold or snowy and galoshes and winter hats and coats were a must. Mom would tie her ever present, babushka (Polish/Russian for head scarf) around her head.

She would bribe us with pennies for the gumball prize machines in the supermarket hallway for only when we were headed home. Walking there was OK, but going home, each of us girls would carry as much as we could handle. Mom carried the heaviest bags with each block seeming longer and longer.

Loaded brown paper bags might get soggy and break if we weren't careful. If ever there were whiney little girls, it would be when we were out of something and had to make a grocery visit on foot.

"The Little Store"…Which is what we called it, was only about three blocks away in a dark and tiny old house on Oak Park Avenue. One little old lady who ran it and sat at the doorway by a cash register every day. The front room area was packed with candy, popsicles, ice cream bars, canned goods, fresh milk and bread. It was down our dirt road and Janice and I were eventually allowed to go there by ourselves in summer when we were a little bit older to buy a Popsicle or candy.

"Living in a country house"…I have to give my mother a lot of credit. She kept a clean house and washed curtains, beddings and floors regularly. She didn't have a clothes dryer until we were in high school. She bought a Hoover vacuum cleaner to clean rugs and floors. That noisy, grey, ugly, alligator looking machine was every housewife's dream come true. She made many attempts at canning fruits and it was too much work for her, so she gave that up. The rest of the fruits we just ate raw as soon as they became ripe. Nothing tastes better than a crunchy

apple right off the tree or fresh raspberries off the bush. But, country living wasn't always picture-perfect.

There were lots of mosquitoes bites in summer and darn those pesky chiggers from the raspberry bushes that got under your skin and were so itchy you went mad. I could lick my finger and just hold it on the welt, but the best remedy was to cover each welt along my waistband with a coat of clear nail polish.

Speaking of home remedies, I cannot forget the ugly brown bottle of Iodine to put on cuts and scrapes. Owww, the painful sting of that smelly stuff! If we hurt ourselves, we didn't want Mom to know so we would be spared the trauma. But she would spot them with her eagle eye. She would snap at me while getting out the smelly, brownish, dreaded Iodine, "Come over here, let me see what happened to your knee?" to which I would reply while pulling away from her, "It's nothing, Mommy, I just scraped it on the sidewalk." She would always grip my little skinny arms with her iron fingers and I never had a choice. When Bactine was finally invented it was such relief. Those were the days.

"Don't feed the squirrels"… Living in the country was quite a learning process for city people. I remember the squirrel I befriended and named Perry. I

made up a story that claimed he was French and worked in our orchard and that I sometimes saw him with a little black beret on his head.

I was always a storyteller even at my tender age, and the most average daily things could take on a second life in my imagination. I would take food out to feed him every day, and he was so cute, eating with his two little paws holding the nuts or cereal. He was always so happy to see me with his little treats. Mom said not to do it anymore, that he was just another wild creature and I dismissed her opinion of my new little friend automatically. Well, I forgot to feed him for a few days.

Then one day when mom went out to hang the laundry to dry on the clothesline, he started stalking her and hissing 'till she ran into the house. She said, "Kathy, it's your fault, I told you not to feed him!" Now he was spitting mad and started jumping on the screen door chattering loudly in a crazed way into the house. All of us closed the door and watched nervously all day from inside until he went away. No more feeding squirrels for me!

"A serious snake incident"... There were occasionally small garter snakes in our backyard, the grown up snakes sometimes measured up to a foot in length. Our house was surrounded by prairie and a golf

course. To be fair, we were on their turf. I wasn't afraid of them because dad showed me how to pick them up. They were harmless and ate insects. One day Mom was washing dishes in the kitchen sink with the window wide open just minding her own business, then Daddy, the jokester that he was, told me to sneak up and put the snake inside the window. Always wanting to please, of course I did as he suggested, and the snake slithered over the sill and into the dishpan full of water. Mom let out a loud shriek and swore at Daddy with words I'd never heard before. Instantly, I knew that had been the wrong thing to do! I whined, "Daddy told me to do it." He said he was sorry in a sheepish way, and I remember mumbling that I wasn't because garter snakes were nothing to be afraid of. Daddy and I both were in the doghouse for a couple of days after that little trick, and Mom never forgot that memorable day.

"My career as the neighborhood mortician"...From the day that I found the first dead bird on the lawn and for every one after, I relished the honor of providing a worthy funeral. The appropriate blooming bush for burial was located and a hole dug. Then a box and lining with soft and colorful fabric to be collected, and I was on my way. I got as many neighborhood kids to stand by and pray at each new

little grave and sometimes talked Mom into standing by even though she expressed her fear of me catching some sort of dread disease. Once each ceremony was over, she would push me to the sink to wash my hands really good and clean with strong soap.

"About mud pies"... Something every little girl should make. Dirt roads in the country are the perfect recipe, mixed with a little rain and stirred with a spoon. We could make the perfect blend for a mud pie feast.

Since there was so little car traffic, after a heavy rain Janice and I would go out together with old tin pie pans and spoons from the kitchen and crouch along side of the road and mix and blend to our hearts content getting grubby with mud and pretending to be master bakers.

Janice always made the best ones and decorated them with pebbles and flowers and still today, I attest that was the beginning of her love of baking and cooking. From mud pie stage to Easy Bake toy ovens and baking sets all the way to today in her grownup kitchen. It has never been an effort for her, just a joy. And her happy place, even today, is in her kitchen, cooking and baking to her heart's content.

"The apple orchard"... Those apple trees were

sometimes so full of apples, we couldn't keep up with them and many fell to the ground and just rotted. It was a big job for all of us. We were always avoiding those pesky wasps and hornets that also loved the sweet rotten apples.

If they were still edible, we would place them in brown paper shopping bags and give them to our friends and neighbors. Some of the more damaged apples were put in a pile, and Dad would throw them at the numerous rabbits and squirrels. He had a great pitching arm and was pretty accurate.

One day he beaned a baby rabbit right on the head and poor Janice cried and thought he killed it. We never found out if the bunny died, but it did disappear. She was so upset she wouldn't speak to him for days and when he was nearby, she would glare at him silently with a serious stink eye. Needless to say, he felt bad and ceased his favorite pastime using our apples to scare away the critters. In looking back, I can't help but consider the symbolism of the apple and the part it has played in my life.

The Happel sisters were teased by neighborhood kids that they were the Apple sisters. It was the apple orchard that was the centerpiece of our magical property.

We climbed those apple trees, hung hammocks from them, picked baskets of apples to bake with, or ate them right off the trees. We didn't need to wash them. We used no pesticides in those days.

To us, dirt was a mud pie word or something to get creative with and dig holes into, not something to be washed off an apple. We just polished the apple on our shirt and took a bite. Is there bacteria on an apple? Heck no, we just needed to look out for an occasional wormhole so we didn't bite into a squirmy worm accidently. There are no words to describe the feeling of picking a ripe apple off a tree on a warm summer day and biting into the crisp, juicy, sweet-tart flesh of it. I could sit in those gnarled branches and dream away the day while munching away on an apple and throw the core as far as I could throw it.

In later years, I looked up "apple" in the Webster Dictionary out of curiosity to try to understand if there was a message in that recurring symbol in relation to our family.

I picture that little house on Argyle Street, and I am once again in the apple orchard. The reference that seems closest to my heart is that apples have long been associated with immortality. If only that were so! My romantic heart likes to believe this notion the most. That is what I picture heaven to be. I know that one day, Grandma, the Happel sisters and all of our loved ones will all meet again in the apple orchard on a beautiful sunny summer day.

"Summer"... Ah, summertime and the living was easy! Now, you have to understand that summertime in the Midwest is so short yet so very sweet because of that. Weather could be cold and windy and even snow up to Easter. With June comes summer vacation from school, and everyone is just itching to get out shorts and bathing suits and get into summertime activities.

We would have ordered some summer clothes from the Sears catalog again and those were waiting, folded neatly until the weather was warm enough to wear. Some years, we had to wait until July for that. Finally, it was time for running around in our yard creating whole worlds of fantasy. We girls were never at a loss for imaginative ideas, and we made up things to do by ourselves. Usually, I could be quite a "Bossy Pants" being three years older than Janice and most of our friends. Mike, Mary Pat, and Ralphie, and Nancy who all lived across the street. We had the biggest yard with lots of trees, and they loved to come to our yard and play. I was introduced at a very young age, right around third grade, to Nancy Drew Mysteries. Mom took my sister and me to a neighborhood toy store, and when I first saw those hardcover mysteries all in a row on the shelf, I had to have one.

Then, I had to have them all. I was hooked from

the first one, and every week I just had to have the next one. Poor Mom, she didn't know what she had started while trying to find something to keep us busy during the hot summer months.

I never could quite picture myself in the role of super sleuths as Nancy and her *boyfriend* Ned Nickerson were, so when I went to look at the next young girls series on the shelf, I came across Cherry Ames and my life took a new path from that day on. Cherry Ames became as familiar and comfortable to me as a best friend. I loved the idea of becoming a nurse and started nursing school in my mind right along with Cherry, as I read each volume intently.

When the setting began to change during World War II, and she became an Army nurse, I became hooked on that romantic time and place. My sister and her friends were so fortunate to have me train them to become nurses right along side of me. HA!

I would set up a tray with sterile utensils — kitchen knife, spoon, Q-tip, rubber band, cake server, cotton balls, manicure scissors, band aids, etc.— for them to memorize just like Cherry had to do and place a white towel over them so they could be tested before their first surgery.

My imagination soared, and they got tired of that game really fast! They moved on to better activities, and I stayed loyal to Cherry, moving up to volume 20 and beyond. I pestered Mom for a real white nurses cap, and she ordered one for me. I was in seventh heaven thinking I could take care of every injury or ailment my family and friends would ever need me for. A little side-note here: After my sons were grown and out of the house, out of curiosity, I looked at the library online and found those books still existed.

At the ripe old age of fifty-five, I requested the first three books and read them with the same feeling of comfort and satisfaction as if the years had hardly passed by. My lifelong love of books has carried me through many stages of my journey, and I am so grateful to have had that luxury.

"The swing set"... We had the neighborhood's first swing set in our yard and the sturdy metal poles and slide became a popular meeting place for exercise, hanging out and trying to top who can swing higher. The seats were wood with metal chains that rusted the first winter and Mikey, our friend from across the street, said that if we got a cut, we would get lockjaw from the rust. We didn't care about any dreaded lockjaw 'cause he probably made it up. I would sit on the swing and dig my feet into the soft muddy rut and twist the chain in a circle as tight as I could, then when it would twist no more, lift my legs straight out and let

it wildly swing in circles and make me dizzy with delight.

My favorite time of day was when the burning sun finally began to set behind the trees after a hot, humid summer day. I could swing high up in air and feel the breeze cool the sweat of the day off me. The sound of the chains became a softer chink and squeak as I gradually slowed to a stop.

"Lightning bugs"...After a full busy day of playing, eating popsicles and dressing dolls, the neighborhood sounds around me changed to a hushed promise of evening as the lightening bugs started their slow blinking signal it was almost time to get ready for bed. Janice and I would get clean jars and pound holes in the top with a nail so the bugs could breath.

We would put a few pieces of grass in the bottom and get busy catching them. We would watch them spark off and on. Mom always made us take off the lids before bed to release them back to nature. She said they would die if we kept them.

One night, I hid the jar under my bed with the lid on and when I woke in the morning, I looked in the jar and almost cried seeing just dry black winged things that looked like ordinary beetles. It was if someone had come in the night and taken the magic right out of them.

Each evening as darkness slowly settled over out little neighborhood, up and down the street I could hear parents shouting for the kids to come home. The last distant hum of a lawn mower finishing as the sun set punctuated the stillness. Oscillating sprinklers gave the lawns a drink before dark with a rhythmic gentle swishing sound over and over. It seemed to me that the whole world was softer and in those moments, I could feel my heartbeat and slowly breathe in the sweet, green summer air.

"Living on the ranch"...During summer vacation our little motley crew with dirty hands and faces would pretend we were Annie Oakley and Roy Rogers and Dale Evans and have a great time enacting scenes from the most popular western TV shows. Ever the drama queen, I even went so far as to tell the younger kids that Roy and Dale actually lived in our attic. I climbed up a ladder into the attic and dragged an old lamp up there and plugged it in, then moved the ladder back.

When they saw a light up there, I think I really convinced them. I told them, the shed in the backyard that resembled a little barn was where Roy and Dale kept their horses, Trigger and Buttercup. There were animal tracks preserved in the cement of our garage that I claimed were footprints of their pets. I think they may have believed me for very short time. I remember how jealous I was that Raymie from across the street had a white and gold toy Roy Rogers rifle, and I pestered him until he let me use it and then I promptly got my thumb caught in the trigger and pinched it badly.

My imagination sure could go wild. My world became limitless and in my mind, I could be anyone and go anywhere. My sister always went along with my stories to my surprise, but then there were those days where we could bicker up a storm but I always knew that we still made quite a team.

If ever she would threaten me with a sassy "I'm telling," I would turn and tell her the made up story that she was really adopted and not really my sister. That would always shut her up really quick. But then, poor Mom had to spend extra time reassuring Janice that it wasn't true at all, while I quickly disappeared, feeling guilty that I had to resort to such wickedness.

"Grubby games"...Running around the trees and hoisting ourselves up into them and dragging things out of the wooden shed was like living in a magic kingdom to us. We pulled out pieces of lumber and moved stuff around all over the yard creating our imaginary world.

Roller-skating was pretty popular and everyone

had a heavy pair of steel roller skates that we would tighten over our shoes with a skate key. Rough, gritty sidewalks with cracks in them were a real challenge, and after skating for a while even when you took off your skates, your feet would still tingle from the vibrations.

We played Tag and Red Rover, and there were lots of shrubs for hide-and-go-seek in if you didn't mind spider webs. We drew chalk marks all over the driveway and sidewalks for hopscotch or sat on the ground for hours with Jacks and marbles. We got really grimy, but I don't ever remember any parent making us wash our hands and faces unless it was "wash your hands before you eat" (with only water if you didn't get caught), a quick wash-up at bedtime or bath time once a week.

Occasionally, one of the moms would wet a washcloth and do a quick swipe at faces as their kids went running by them squirming just out of reach. We were allowed to spend the day doing whatever we wanted and usually ran around looking like little ragamuffins with dirt-streaked faces.

"Secrets"...Each day after Mom cleaned up the house, she would take her break and read her beloved Romance magazines. She would read the short stories in Real Romance and True Story and keep them

hidden where she thought we couldn't find them. After I began to read better, I wondered what she was so interested in reading and would sneak a peek and read what I could before Janice would catch me and complain, "You aren't supposed to be reading them, I'm gonna tell Mom!" That was the beginning of many times during my pre-teen years that she "became the boss over me."

When I was in eighth grade, Mom began to trust me to walk to go "shopping" with a friend. Instead, I would sneak off to spend time at the local roller skating rink "The Hub" and run back by my summer curfew at 9PM. I finally broke the sisterly power she had over me with a meeting behind a locked door in the bathroom, which made me feel guilty so I ended up not sneaking around anymore.

"Everyone is invited"...Summer time was also the best season to have BIG parties. Our backyard was a full city block long and to my parents it seemed that we could invite hundreds of guests. Mom and Dad went to all sorts of effort to put those parties together. Daddy was a master of sports, and he put up a professional volleyball net, and we had very competitive Badminton and Volleyball games punctuated with squeals and laughter, dramatic pratfalls and tumbles.

There was croquet and horseshoes, hula-hoop contests and lots of dancing. He got a big box of College Team pennants on swags of rope to hang around the yard from tree to tree. Alas, there was free flowing beer and plenty of hard liquor, and at almost every party, someone would fall into the 3-foot Doughboy pool with their clothes on.

Also, there was always music. I can remember some of those songs as the soundtrack of my life. I still can hear those melodies in a far corner of my mind echoing in the dark as they played them at the many parties we had with friends and family through the years. *On The Sunny Side of the Street* was a family favorite, and Daddy taught my sister and I to sing it with him, each of us parked on one of his knees apiece, crooning our little hearts out. As we belted out the tune, our life seemed so sweet and as children, there were no worries to leave on anyone's doorstep, but oh, how we loved to sing that song together. Mommy and Daddy loved to hear it over and over again.

In my mind, there is nothing like the sound of the sweet trumpet of Harry James or Glenn Miller's pure instrumental harmonies that can trigger a sudden feeling of homesickness. And that "Ol' Blue Eyes" Frank Sinatra, well, we heard a lot of him. Mom and Dad played that music when anyone dropped in for a visit and to play Scrabble or cards.

The bigger the group the louder the singing, and they would put on the Mitch Miller Sing-Along albums and pass out lyric sheets for all to sing. "You Are My Sunshine" was a song that became a family standard to sing for generations and was the first lullaby to sing to each new baby born to us in coming years. My sister and I knew the words and harmonies by heart to all of those songs and even as we grew much older, we would sing them again with old age scratchy voices, smiling in remembrance.

One of the biggest parties was the Luau. Mom was ever creative with themes but Hawaiian style was her biggest hit. We made gobs of tissue paper flowers and hung streamers. Mom made a giant poster of a life-sized Hawaiian girl dancing the Hula. In those days, there were no artistic shortcuts to look at pictures for inspiration, so she hand sketched it and painted it with poster paints, dressed her in a hula skirt and topped her off with a flower Lei and tacked her to the wooden gate post.

Everyone came dressed Hawaiian style and once again, they brought out to the patio the Portable Hi-Fi that played 33 1/3 RPM records. They had quite a collection of records but added Island music to the mix of favorites in the stack of albums for that party.

I can still see their faces and hear the laughter at the parties that would go from afternoon to dark when the last romantic sounds of the Harry James Orchestra could be heard softly on a moonlit night. "I've Heard That Song Before" and "You Made Me Love You," with the last fading trumpet notes soaring skyward. You could almost feel the darkness at the end of the orchard moving softly closer as the scent of sweet apples would flood the soft summer night until all of the guests wandered home again and sleepy children were carried home to their beds.

"Autumn"...Every year, the trees were stripped bare of summertime as they shivered in the cold air getting ready for winter. We had a small orchard of thirteen apple trees, three cherry trees, two plum trees, grapevines, and multitude of shrubs. Daddy, Janice, and I would rake and pile up the crunchy carpet of leaves.

Then, he would have us stand back as he lit a match to the pile until wisps of smoke and flames licking at the dried leaves would cut into the sharp cold air. It was a strangely bitter, yet a sweet, smoldering aroma. The flickering flame of the bonfire pile of autumn leaves was a sight to behold. In those days, everyone used to burn leaves in the yards of their homes. Daddy would watch over the fire carefully, as carefully as he would watch over his precious daughters over the years.

We three were strangely silent and apart in our own thoughts bundled up against the crisp air watching as the smoke and tiny sparks swirled up into the overcast skies. Summer over; back in school; winter coming; the past receding farther into our memories. The nostalgic yearly "Indian Summer" color illustration had just come out in the Chicago Sun-Times newspaper depicting just that, as the hazy smoke sparked our imaginations as summer drew to a close.

Each day became shorter and darkness crept in right around dinnertime. We would have a little family TV time just before bed. My sister, never wanting to miss a thing, would beg to stay up just a little later. I would always argue, "What's the point of her staying up later, she always falls asleep right away watching TV anyways." But once Janice fell asleep, Daddy would pick her up and safely tuck her into bed.

Bedtime was always a hug and kiss from my parents and a "Ja Cie Kocham" in Polish meaning "I love you." Mom then fell asleep while watching TV and eventually shuffled, half asleep, to bed. Daddy would be the last one to turn out the lights of our little house going room to room checking door locks, turning off the TV and then each light. Outside our window, the cold wind would send the dry branches of leafless bushes and trees scratching along the side of the house while within, the reassuring hum of the furnace would warm our rooms as we snuggled safely under our blankets. *Pleasant dreams little family.*

"Winter"...As a child, winter was my magical time. All my sister and I could think about was how many weeks until Christmas. We would lay on the floor for hours going over the Sears Christmas catalog circling the things we wanted most in hopes Santa would be generous each year.

Right after Thanksgiving, Mom would take us on the bus and then the El, the elevated train that went above and then underground to the final destination downtown, to go to Marshall Fields and Carson Pirie Scott to look at the windows full of toys displayed in Christmas fantasy settings. There were moving figures of Santa, Elves and Fairies and always a train going around. We pressed our little faces against those windows in absolute yearning to see the details as close as we could as we steamed up the window with our breath. Even when I got older, I would go with girlfriends to carry on the downtown tradition, minus pressing my nose against the glass, of course.

Every year, the whole family gathered again at Auntie Nancy's house to see Grandma for Christmas. Each of the cousins (but not the four boys) would get to pick a new crocheted lace hankie from Grandma. Of course, we all sang Christmas carols and Grandma Carrie sure loved it when Daddy sang them in Polish.

Daddy and Grandma would always get tears in their eyes and even though we didn't understand the words in Polish, we got tears in our eyes, too. Then came the year that my cousins Ronnie, Randy and Roxanne, the 3 R's, got a 45rpm record by Alvin and the Chipmunks "Christmas Don't Be Late." And they played it over and over, and over at least 40 times with the sound turned on LOUD. That was a really memorable year! 'Till this day at Christmas, Alvin still wants his hula-hoop!

The day Daddy brought home a real Christmas tree found us hopping and skipping around in such excitement. Each year, Mom usually thought the tree was much too skinny and had too many bare spaces, but we all got busy hanging thread after thread of crinkly silver lead icicles on every inch after the string of big red, green, blue and gold glass bulb lights was placed among the branches. It transformed our tree into a beauty to behold with a little love and attention.

There weren't any ornaments, but when we plugged in the lights, the reflections on all of the tinsel was a glowing magical sight. Janice and I would sit at the bottom of the tree and walk our little fingers through the branches and pretend we lived in the little shimmering, colored spaces wherever there was a tinsel gap.

Then came the momentous year when we were in our teens. Mom saw the new style of the silver aluminum Christmas trees with golden satin covered foam balls, and her heart took a sudden u-turn. She just had to have one of those trees. Beneath the tree, there was a whirring, revolving glass disc with red, green, blue, and gold glass to reflect on the tree and change the shimmering tree in a way that felt like we were being hypnotized as we watched it change from color to color.

A couple of years of that and then, came the artificial green tree to put together but never again a real green tree in our house. When Mom wanted to sell the old silver tree at the Harlem Outdoor Movie Theater swap meet, there were other spindly silver trees leaning crookedly by each booth in a sad way but no one would even pay a quarter for them.

The first year in our new home in Elk Grove Village, Glenn and I bought our first real tree again. When we got it home and smelled the spicy pine scent, I couldn't help the unexpected tears that fell along with the sudden rush of memories. Hello, old friend. I sighed, as I buried my face into the branches with the piney scent of my childhood.

Most of my winter memories revolve around the freezing cold, icicles and the snow. Icicles hung from the roof all around the little house on Argyle Street, sometimes so big and thick, we would have to break them off so they didn't pull off the house gutters with their weight.

In the daytime, you could hear the steady drip, drip, drip as they started to melt, only to freeze again in the night. The life cycle of the icicle was always a mystery to me. Though beautiful in their crystal glory especially shining in the sun, their lifespan was so short.

Shoveling snow was a constant memory. We took turns shoveling the driveway so dad could pull the car in when he came home. After the first four years of living in our little house, our neighborhood finally grew up and streets were paved, sidewalks put in, and street lights to chase the dark nights away. I remember looking up at the street lights standing with my snow shovel and seeing snow flurries coming down illuminated by the light behind, all falling softly to the ground. It gave me such a feeling of aloneness as the world around me began to fade away.

It's hard to explain to someone who has never lived in a cold climate that even the smell of snow is not like any other. If you breathe the air through your nose right before an expected snowfall, there is a crispness mixed with a subtle heavy dampness that prompts one to remark, "Smells like snow coming."

As the flurries begin, sounds become more muffled and signs of other people and cars disappear as the snow becomes heavier. Aside from the beauty, there was also the harsher side of winter. The freezing cold, often well below 0 degrees with a "Wind Chill Factor," which only meant colder than the temperature! One freezing day, I overheard Daddy tell Mom in the kitchen when he came in, "It's colder out there than a witches tit!" To which she quickly admonished, "Casey, quiet! The girls might hear you!" I heard and never did forget that one.

Ice storms were the scary ones —windy, with little needles of ice to peck at your bare face if it was uncovered. The street would be full of icy ruts and many times cars got stuck in them. I remember the sound of spinning, grating, frozen tires trying to get out of a rut to no avail. Mom or Dad would go out to try to give those strangers a push from the rear to get them out again.

Cars would skid all over the roads no matter which way the driver turned the wheel and many car accidents happened because of it. We had to spread salt over walkways so we wouldn't slip and kill ourselves just to get into the house. The ice would coat the brittle branches of our trees and sometimes they would crash to the ground from the weight of the ice along with high winds. The cold could be painful at times and no amount of bundling up would protect us from it. Your eyes would water, and the frosty breath from your nose and mouth would freeze on even the thickest scarf wrapped around your face.

"Snow days"...Were what we prayed for and would listen to the radio early in the morning for school closures holding our breath until we heard St. Monica School announced and then there were no happier children than we.

The rest of the winter was a never ending row of galoshes, (rubber boots) in the basement of St. Monica School. My sister and I had fur trim at the top of each boot to distract from the ugly big zippers, and we wore them over our shoes. Daddy had men's rubber boots with clanking metal fasteners. Poor Mom with no drier for her laundry still hung clothes out on a clothesline in the yard. Quite often when they froze solid, she would take them down in solid hard chunks and lay them on a wooden clothes rack next to the furnace to defrost and finally dry.

"Sick days"...Chicago winters were not for the tender hearted. Once November was over, our little ugly, dented tin vaporizer would always be plugged in for a steady stream of hissing steam. It was rusty little pot but it reassured our parents that we would be safe

from the dreaded *Pneumonia*. I loved Luden's cherry cough drops and ate a whole box at a time. Crunching them with my teeth so the noise drove mom crazy.

Also a favorite and much more silent, were the rubbery Pine Brothers cherry or honey cough drops. I would put five or six in my mouth at one time for a full jolt of flavor. It was a time of colds and sore throats, which my sister and I had often. We stayed home on sick days too many times to count, and I think Mom enjoyed having our company. Sometimes even if my sister wasn't sick, she would keep us both home and vice versa. Our report cards had so many days always exceeding double digits, marked in the column "Out Sick."

The smell of Vicks Vapor Rub was a common odor that time of year in many homes. It was a sharp, spicy menthol scent and when it was rubbed into your skin, it had a warm burning sensation. The smell of Vicks always managed to evoke the feeling of being taken care of when we were feeling poorly.

At the first sign of a sniffle, it would be rubbed under our noses and all over our chests and back. If there were a cough, Daddy would give us a teaspoon of that icky sticky stuff to swallow. Years later, we came to find out that Vicks Vapor Rub taken internally was a toxic and possible dangerous thing to do. It was in very small print on the label of the jar, but who knew? We still survived.

We really never went to the doctor unless one of us was very sick. A walk to see old Dr. Haupt on Higgins avenue was a fearsome thing indeed. He had a heavy German accent and if we were there, it only meant we had to lower our heavy, noisy corduroy pants from our little butts and get a shot, which struck fear in our hearts for both Janice and I.

When the polio scare began, Mom marched us in to see Dr Haupt once again while gripping our little shoulders with an iron fist and a stern warning, "No whining, you have to get that Polio shot!" There were no happier girls than we when the vaccine began to be distributed on a sugar cube instead.

"How to pass the time on a cold, dark winter day"...Winter was the time for board games and we had *Chutes and Ladders* and *Candyland*. Later, we had *The Barbie Game*, *Clue*, *Monopoly*, and a cool dimensional *Haunted House* game. We both hated ugly *Mr. Potato Head*! Winter meant staying inside most of the time and playing with our dolls. I loved all of my dolls. I had my *Revlon Doll* with real pierced diamond teardrop earrings, and a *Toni Doll*.

Janice had a nun doll and bride doll. I remember the year that the original *Barbie* doll was born. That was a vivid eye opener because all of the moms debated in whispers if she was to busty and lusty looking for their young and tender daughters.

My sister Janice wasn't crazy about dolls and thought they were useless unless they had a persona, such as the nun or bride or orphan. Mine were strictly fashion dolls with no purpose. I loved to dress them up and accessorize. Mom sewed doll clothes by hand for us to expand their wardrobes.

I would trim their hair into ragged edges with my safety scissors and comb in VO5 to enhance it, only making it a sticky mess. I changed their lip color with nail polish, and it got gummy while fuzz and lint stuck to it and looked pretty bad. I even borrowed mom's blue eye shadow once to put on their eyelids and when I tried to wipe it off with a tissue, the skin colored paint came right off with it. They ended up pretty creepy looking by the time I was done with them.

Janice wanted a *Pitiful Pearl* doll one Christmas and her heart went out to that poor little doll. The description was a sad little orphan doll dressed in rags. Mom didn't get it for her and Santa didn't leave one under the tree. My sister was so disappointed when her friend got one and not her; I think it broke her heart. I guess sometimes parents don't always know what's good for us.

"Pack in the people, it's time to party"...As the year grew toward its end and the daylight was at its shortest, dark nights were so long, and a bright spot to look forward to was the annual Christmas parties for friends and neighbors. The menu typically was Christmas cookies, pretzels and chips with Lipton Onion Soup dip, and free flowing beer and hard liquor.

Also on the bar menu was Mom's famous Christmas Cocktail with raw egg, powdered sugar and gin topped with cream soda and whipped up for the ladies. What a glowing, hugging, singing group we were. One bedroom was full of coats piled high to the top of the windows with a couple of the littlest kids sleeping between the coats by the end of the evening.

My all time favorite of winter memories was a tradition started when I was around 7 years old until I was married when the passage of time began to unravel our traditions. Each Christmas morning after breakfast and all the kids on the block had opened the presents Santa had brought, we would begin.

First, one family would start the caravan going to the second house all bundled up and singing to the next house picking up that family, and so on singing Christmas carols, parents and children alike.

Even a snapping cold Christmas day would not stop us from going house to house, until we reached the last house on the block. We always went to each back door, because a large group of people with snowy boots to remove and drip on floors went to the kitchen door first so it was easier to clean up the mess.

At each house, the parents would go in and would raise a glass to toast Merry Christmas, often in their own family language of those loved ones who came before and we all joined in to celebrate together. From a melting pot of differences and similarities those wishes came, flowing freely and sometimes with tears in our eyes, feeling sheltered in the love of our friends.

Wesoiych Swiat: Polish, Buon Natale: Italian, Frohliche Weihnachten: German, Joyeux Noel: French, and then Dad would close the toasting at that last house with "Na Zdrowie" in Polish meaning "To your health," and then he sang in his fine voice with tears in his eyes, *"Stolat, Stolat"* with everyone joining in, the song wishing "May you live 100 years!"

9

"The Golden Age Of Television"

How lucky we were to have a television in our home. My parents never bought anything on credit. "If you can't pay for it, you don't need it." It took time to save up all that money. We got our first Philco TV housed in a big solid wood cabinet for around $400.00. That was a fortune in those days! I was only around four years old when Daddy bought that first television, but I loved watching it! The screen was only a 15-inch circle and of course it was only black and white. Daddy would stretch out along the floor in front of it, the closer the better to see it. In those days, the men's fashions were baggy pleated pants with a narrow leather belt to hold them up and his loose change would always fall out from his pockets onto the rug. I would find coins and hide them thinking I was rich indeed. There was a bunny ears antenna on top to adjust the clarity of the picture.

Mom and Dad's favorites were *I Love Lucy* and *The Jackie Gleason Show*. They loved to see the performances of their favorite singers on *The Perry Como Show* and *The Lucky Strike Hit Parade*. There was that dark crime show, *Dragnet* with Detective Joe Friday. At the beginning of each show the announcer would say *"Ladies and gentlemen, the story you are about to see is true. The names have been changed to protect the innocent."* After the end of each evening's broadcast, as the station went off the air, an announcer would close the evening programming and the national anthem would play. Then, a loud piercing sound would come on the screen with the logo to let you know the end of broadcasting for the day. Many times Daddy had fallen asleep on the floor I would awake in my bed and hear that sound until he would finally turn off the set and go to bed.

I can still remember so clearly when Janice and I were a little older. We saw the first version of *Peter Pan* the musical play that was broadcast on television. It was televised in black and white as all shows were at that time. We sat on the floor right in front of the set so immersed in the story of the little boy who never grew up. Mary Martin sang such a beautiful heartfelt song that the words and melody have stayed in my mind for my entire life. I have tried to sing it to myself on occasion when I'm alone, and always by the end, tears spring to my eyes before the last familiar notes. Sometimes, I can't finish the last few lines, especially the part, *"you can never, never grow old."* What a magical, mystical place is Neverland, but I guess you must find it in your heart after all...

As the years went by, the first Color TV was the biggest family event for us. I remember neighbors stopping by just to sneak a peek. I can still remember my sister and I sprawled out on the rug in front of the TV watching our favorite shows, *Mighty Mouse, Huckleberry Hound, Casper the Friendly Ghost,* and the more serious *Kukla, Fran and Ollie, Romper Room, Garfield Goose,* and of course, *Bozo's Circus.*

About the time that I was just about ready to start first grade, a new television program started called *Disneyland.* Walt Disney, who seemed like a likable uncle to his television audience, would point out on a big wall map introducing us to each area in his new park in California that would be opening soon. It seemed so magical to visit Frontierland, Fantasyland, or Tomorrowland through each week's new segment. Even though black and white, my imagination began to soar, especially when Davy Crockett came on the screen. Every kid, including myself got a coonskin cap to wear around the neighborhood. We would reenact the episodes.

One day, I asked Mom if we could go to the new Disneyland when it opened and she said it was too far, almost on the other side of the world so we never

could go. To us at that time, California did seem
unreachable. When *Mickey Mouse Club* began, I
discovered my new favorite show. Those dancing and
singing Mouseketeers were my idols. I loved the series
Spin and Marty, but gosh, I was so jealous of Annette.
She seemed to have everything a young girl could ever
want.

Then with our first color Television, *Walt
Disney's Wonderful World Of Color* really gave us
something to be inspired by. I always wanted to go to
Disneyland and never imagined that one day I would
live just down the road from there and have annual
passes to come and go as we please as if we belonged
there. Talk about a dream come true. I even worked at
the Disneyland Hotel for a brief time. I have never
tired of the Disney "Magic," and it has continued to
feed my imagination from my very earliest memories
and well into my old age.

Those early television years cultivated in me
my budding romantic nature. I adored *Adventures in
Paradise* and *Sky King*. When *Ozzie and Harriet, My
Three Sons, Father Knows Best,* and *The Donna Reed
Show* came on, Mom and Dad joined us and then we
really had family TV night! I was in heaven watching
how boys act in a family by seeing Paul Peterson, and
Ricky Nelson (sigh), grow up with me. Forget *Leave It
To Beaver* though. Beaver was so annoying! What

kind of parent calls their son by the nickname of Beaver?

For a real treat, we would eat our TV dinners on a folding metal TV tray as we watched our shows. Variety shows were my parent's favorite. *The Ed Sullivan Show*, *The Perry Como Show,* and *Andy Williams Show* (I'll never forget those adorable Osmonds) entertained us as we sat glued to the set enjoying all of the new songs and talent together.

My early preteen years brought a new reality to my love of music, and now I was able to enjoy the music and watch new dance crazes on *American Bandstand*. Every day at around 4:00pm, I would sit in front of the TV set waiting for the familiar Bandstand intro-music waiting to see some of my favorite songs performed by the artists. I got to know the "regular" couples by name. There was Justine and Bob and Arlene and Kenny, seen together week after week coming directly into my living room from Philadelphia. Dick Clark became a well known to me as my own family.

'Til today, some of the opening songs and nostalgic closing songs of the shows still sometimes run through my mind like a distant memory. Engraved in my subconscious are the songs sounding as they did when I was falling asleep after the last show with the tune still humming in my head.

I could hear from my room that sweet song by Andy Williams at the closing of every show: "May Each Day Of Your Life Be A Good Day," and then he wished that the Lord always watch over us. What more could we ask for after all. *"Good Night Andy..."*

10

School Days

Daddy went to Holy Innocents Catholic Elementary School, and the thing he wanted most was to have us go to a Catholic school at all costs. St. Monica Church and School was a six-block walk from our house, "close enough," in Daddy's eyes. There are so many memories attached to that school and church. In the Catholic school system, many children didn't go to kindergarten in those days and just started in first grade. For me, it was exciting, until I realized I was but one little girl in a class of 50 other students under the supervision of one stern nun. The school was run by an order of nuns, "The Sisters of Mercy" by name. There were many nuns from Ireland in that order and their soft Irish brogue would sometimes sneak into their conversations. At first, I was suspicious of their strange long black habits with their hair covered by veils, but they were a nurturing group of women in spite of their thankless task of teaching an unruly pack of children daily for the rest of their lives.

The first week of school was the time to check out all the kids that would be in your classroom and decide which ones had the "cooties" and which ones were "really neat." Boys usually had "cooties" because they picked their noses and ignored us girls. The girls had about one week to wear our new fall fashions before the deadline date that uniforms had to be worn. And each day, much attention was placed on each outfit. It was also a time to get out Mom's brown paper grocery bags that she saved to cover all of our textbooks to keep the books clean. I hated the measuring and folding and taping. If it wasn't done nicely enough, you could get in trouble and Sister would tell you to take it home to re-do it.

Picture long straight rows of desks where students usually were seated alphabetically unless you were a "problem kid," then you had to be moved in front so Sister could keep an eye on you.

I was always in the back because I was a W for Weglarz. A Polish name that no one would even try to pronounce. There were lots of other Polish names in the class, but they almost all ended in ski. Everyone wore a uniform. In the early years, the boys wore a dark green dress shirt. Then when they reached the upper grades, the uniforms changed to a beige cotton dress shirt with a strange little brown tie and dark pants. They all looked totally *blah*.

Unfortunately for the girls, our uniforms stayed the same for all of the eight years at St Monica's. We wore a heavy, dark green jumper that came to the middle of our shin and white cotton socks folded neatly at the ankle. There was a little yellow-gold embroidered emblem "SMS" on the jumper, representing Saint Monica School.

We wore a white cotton short sleeve blouse under the jumper, and Mom hated to wash and iron them so she didn't very often. When the laundry got backed up, I would go get the plastic bag from the refrigerator with some of my extra school blouses all rolled up, starchy, damp and ready to iron and hand it over to Mom.

There was rarely a physical education class or sports, but in spring, we would get to go out on the blacktop playground (which was just the church parking lot) for recess and run around and get sweaty. Sometimes, the nuns would organize races for exercise. By eighth grade, we could compete for a yearly race for the GAA, Girls Athletic Association. We got to wear a little gold pin on our uniform if we passed the time testing for races. I was a fast runner with long skinny legs, so I passed and got my pin.

In the classroom, the nuns were supreme. With all of the nuns living in the convent on the corner of the parking lot, we didn't get away with much even when we would hang around the playground after school. They would always know what we were up to. Each day when Sister called the classroom to order, we would stand and place our hand over our heart and recite the Pledge of Allegiance. Then, we all had to sit with our hands folded on our desktop in a prayerful manner and no talking during classes.

We had two bathroom breaks a day, and we would line up outside the restroom door to take our turn in one of four stalls in each boys or girls bathrooms. It took a while for us to get through those lines. There was always a bathroom monitor to report any suspect behavior. Poor Bob got in trouble once for brushing his teeth at the bathroom sink and was told that was something to do only at home.

If you couldn't wait until bathroom break time, you could raise your hand, and every eye in the classroom would turn to you as you explained that you had to go to the bathroom, NOW. Sometimes Sister would be in the middle of something important, and you would have to wait and squirm around hoping you could make it in time. As a result, sometimes there were classroom accidents that could not be avoided, much to the embarrassment of the student and would result as a black mark on your reputation forever.

Rules, rules, and more rules. It was always so hard for me to sit still, and I usually got regular reminders to stop fidgeting. It also was so hard to stay awake while sitting in the same uncomfortable little desk for almost the whole day long except for lunch and recess. I was a compulsive daydreamer, and one glance out the windows was enough to send my imagination as well as my attention soaring away.

The students were a melting pot of different nationalities, and we all knew who was what. Italian, Polish, German, but mostly Irish, for St. Monica's parish was an Irish parish, and many of the priests and nuns came from Ireland or their parents had. Father's McCabe and Guerin and all of the nuns at the convent took their vocations seriously, but especially the nuns, for there were no other assistants or classroom helpers for those poor ladies.

I can remember a series of old black and white movies that seemed like a mirror of our old fashioned Catholic school life, *Going My Way* and *The Bells of St. Mary's* with that gentle crooner Bing Crosby who starred as a priest and Ingrid Bergman, that sweetest of nuns. Those movies sure bring back so many memories of my days at school.

The Sisters were stern taskmasters so in order to make peace out of chaos, they improvised and punishments were allowed and could be quite creative. Sister Elise, in seventh grade, struck fear in our hearts if we got assigned to her classroom. What a tough tyrant she was. She was of a chubby stature and shorter than most of the boys but VERY strong.

If you saw her rolling toward you down the aisle at warp speed, all eyes would pop open in fear that your desk would be her destination. A bar of soap in the mouth of Jack, A smack with a wooden ruler on the hand of Bob, A wooden pointer over the shoulder of Judson, but *"thank God"* the girls usually escaped with a tongue lashing or public ridicule. Vinette was one girl that was always getting the stink-eye from Sister Elise, but Vinette was very tough indeed, as most of the Italians were. I always admired her for her fearlessness.

There were also a few fearless boys that no threat of a smacking of a ruler had any effect on. For those most unruly ones, Sister would get up close, grab the ear, and lift them out of their desk with a sudden jerking movement, walk them to the principal's office. Needless to say we were all pretty much in fear of punishment or embarrassment and we always knew who was the boss. Yes Sister, or no Sister was the respectful response to any questions. If anyone got in trouble in school, the parents would pick it up from there when they got home and add more punishment. The Sisters were always right, even when they weren't. No amount of excuses would get us off the hook.

My sister Janice was more sensitive than I and from her first day of school, her heart was struck with fear. Those serious looking nuns dressed in black from head to toe with not a human hair showing seemed alien to her. She was used to being alone with Mom every day for the three years after I started school, so the shock of first grade turned her into an official runaway.

I was called out of my classroom to search for my missing sister at least three times at the beginning of that year with everyone in a panic, but she was always found back at home. It was a difficult time for her being separated from Mom, and she was afraid of Nuns forever after.

On the wall outside the entrance to our school was a bold yellow and black sign representing a Nuclear Shelter. During one of my elementary school years was the Cuban Missile Crisis. That was a frightening era of air raid warnings once again that our post-war generation had not ever experienced. During that short time, we had regular duck and cover drills in dark hallways, in the basements, and under desks. The terror of a nuclear bomb cutting short our lives at any time was something that we never got used to. When that problem was finally resolved, the deep sighs of relief were felt by everyone. I have always prayed to God that we never have to worry about that again.

Some of the most memorable things about school for me are probably the same for any other Catholic school student from my era. The curriculum was a cookie cutter similarity from school to school, with no room for change for many years. I found that whenever I met someone in my later years that went to Catholic school around the same time as I did, they had almost the exact same stories of fears and embarrassments or incidents to laugh at. I find that concept comforting and yet disturbing if I could use those two descriptions in the same breath. But don't ask me to explain why I say that. I couldn't explain, even if I tried.

In my earliest recollection of second grade we had a special holiday assembly to watch *Miracle on 34th Street* shown on a roll up screen with a scratchy projector to start the season off on the right foot.

All of the students and their teachers sat in the auditorium for those two hours on uncomfortable metal folding chairs, where of course I swung my feet and fidgeted too much, so Sister Raphael made me sit by her. Oh the embarrassment, but that movie was so magical. I still believe in Santa Claus.

Every year when the countdown to Christmas began at school it was time to sell Christmas cards as a school fundraiser. The excitement of the season with decorations on the bulletin boards decorated for

Christmas was a daily reminder. For Advent, we would light a candle in the classroom on a real pine advent wreath and sing the Christmas Carols in our piping high-pitched voices. Out of her voluminous pocket, Sister Raphael would take out the round shiny silver pitch pipe to give us a start. We sang one in Latin as we were taught, "Adeste Fideles" but the best was always "Silent Night." We would sing as if our hearts were soaring like the angels.

Sister would tell us that was just what we sounded like with a twinkle in her eye as the last notes finally dwindled. At that magical time of year, we each felt closer to both baby Jesus and Santa Claus equally, and those tiny seeds took root in our little childish hearts.

I can still recall many elaborate church occasions to celebrate the sacraments. First of all, let me share that I loved the Latin Mass, as I had experienced during my years at St. Monica Church. It is just a personal preference and opinion, of course. There was something mystical of a mass said in Latin as it had been for centuries by followers of Christ. It moved me to a time and place where religion first began and gave me an essence of that time and a peacefulness that would allow serious contemplation about faith and goodness. Somehow, my prayers seemed more holy.

Combined with the ethereal Gregorian Chant music—I loved singing in the choir—and the scent of incense, that time in church seemed to connect me to the faith of my father and those before him for so many centuries. Even with it's pomp and circumstance, it just felt so comfortable to me.

All right then, let me continue on to my religious rites of passage. In second grade, my First Holy Communion, where all the girls got dressed up in fancy white dresses and a white veil just like a little bride. Oh, I was so proud of my pretty lace dress and veil along with new shoes with a tiny heel that I wore on that day. We had a party at our house after the ceremony with Holy Communion cake. All the family came over and gave me cards with money in them.

Third grade was the year that I decided that I would spell my name Kathy with an "ie" because there were at least five other Kathy's in the third grade. That was my first move toward individuality and once bitten, I always chose the path less taken forever more.

Then a few years later, in fifth grade, I had my Confirmation. We wore choir robes, no party, no cake here, lots of pomp and circumstance, but no money in cards. My Cousin Karen was my Sponsor, and she was there by my side through the long service at church. One girl named Patsy fainted and hit her head on the hard marble floor and was bleeding all over, so that made the service even longer when they had to carry her out. It was hot in those long robes, and I hoped and prayed I would not embarrass myself the same way.

Catholics pick a Saints name for every sacrament to add to their birth name, so by Confirmation time I became Kathleen Virginia Mary Veronica. I chose the name Veronica because I was a big fan of the Archie comics and Veronica with the long dark hair was my idol. I hoped there was a saint by that name and finally found one. What a long drawn out moniker for a small, skinny little girl!

In sixth grade, I learned about politics. I began to hear my parents talk about a man called John Fitzgerald Kennedy. It was a time when I started to watch the news and "Jack" and his wife, Jackie Kennedy, were always in the news. What a fairytale family they seemed, and at school, all of the nuns almost swooned in their interest, because not only was he young and handsome, but the first Irish Catholic to boot. And, the priests and nuns who lived in the convent and rectory were almost all Irish, so who do you think they favored?

During election time, we were allowed to wear "Vote for Kennedy" buttons on our uniforms, even though no jewelry other than holy medals and scratchy wool scapulars (to remind us to do penance for our sins) were allowed. We all prayed that JFK would win the election and when he did, everyone was so jubilant, for that November in 1961, our prayers were answered!

In seventh grade, we had a class in hygiene with boys in one room and girls in the other. We were reminded to bathe more often because we were changing into adults and should wear deodorant. The girls were given a small discreet paper booklet to take home and read. That was the extent of the class about growing up to be an adult soon. No other questions were allowed, but if someone was bold enough to ask, they were told to either see Sister after class, or ask your parents. Obviously, no one wanted to see Sister after class and we certainly didn't want to ask our parents so that was the end of that. Some of the girls including myself started to shave our legs and that was a traumatic experience, and we whispered to each other about that and other changes with blushing faces.

That year, we had a school play, "Snow White." All of our sweaty bodies were crammed on to a tiny stage in the assembly hall and sang "Some Day My Prince Will Come" to my heart's delight. Also we sang "Whistle While You Work," with plenty of off pitch whistling, and other songs from that movie.

I think we felt we were certainly on the way to being Broadway stars. We were one big chorus in rows filling the stage because there were one hundred students in that year's seventh grade class as we moved up toward our graduation.

Eighth grade was a most memorable year for me because I got a transistor radio for my birthday that summer before school started. I suddenly felt so grown up. It was the size of a cigarette package—which was a common household accessory at that time—and a shade of pale robin's egg blue. I would walk around holding it to my ear wherever I went. WLS and WCFL were the main stations I listened to and Dick Biondi my favorite announcer, but Wolfman Jack was a wild and crazy alternate. I placed my transistor radio under the edge of my pillow each night and fell asleep to music until one day my dad told me if I kept doing that, I would wear out the batteries and they were too expensive.

The Beach Boys were my big favorite with "Surfer Girl" and Jan and Dean's "Surf City." The Ventures song, "Wipe Out" was so fine! I could transport myself along with the radio waves to sunny California waves never knowing that someday I would live there. But when I heard Bobby Vinton sing "Blue Velvet," I dreamed of what it was going to be like when I was in high school and on the way my first romance. Top songs from another group, the Four Seasons, hit the top of the charts week after week while the music went round and round.

"Springtime"...Easter marked the beginning of spring each year, but usually it was still cold and could even snow. My mother honored the Easter tradition of getting an Easter dress and hat for all of us girls each year. Easter shoes and a little purse rounded each carefully chosen outfit, and we would dress for church hoping and praying that we didn't have to wear our winter coat over our new spring finery.

When the air was finally warming up, we watched for tender Crocus, Jonquils, and Tulips as they began pushing their faces up toward the warm sun in the yard, signaling that the long winter was finally over.

"Church Carnival"...St. Monica held it's yearly church carnival just before the end of the school year. Hallelujah! The excitement became contagious, and all that the boys and girls could talk about was "The Carnival!" There was a Ferris wheel, Tilt-a-whirl, and lots of food booths and carnival games run by parents. I always loved the little plastic yellow ducks floating around a water path you could pick up and possibly win a prize if there was a number on the bottom. I never won anything, but loved those cute little yellow ducks.

I begged permission to go with a group of my

school friends and just "hang out" acting so cool and giving the eye to all the guys. Girls only talked to girls, and guys only talked to the guys, for fear of *sin*. We just giggled and looked at the boys while they ran around doing the things that boys do, mostly gross in our opinion. More than that would have landed us in the confession booth. Heaven have mercy!

By the end of eighth grade, we had all developed an inventory of what we learned about *SIN* through our elementary school years. One of the first sins we were concerned about in our childish, confused state was, "You can't wear black patent leather shoes because boys could see up your skirt in the reflection from them." Then we considered the possible consequences of, "Don't ever touch a person of the opposite sex because that might be leading them to sinful thoughts."

For girls in eighth grade, a dire warning for our future once we leave the safety of our beloved St. Monica, "No dining in places with white tablecloths with a boy because it would remind our dates of white bed sheets." This one was particularly confusing to us.

Another common BIG sin was no swearing, including the dreaded sh_t, cr_p, or da_n! Now, here we go folks, even with a missing letter I think you can figure out which words were a sin to confess to Father Guerin on Friday. If in doubt, you could always just say, "Bless me Father for I have sinned, I said a bad word two times," and hope he would be lenient and give you a small penance without asking what the word was, because just to repeat it to him was a sin again. In elementary school, most of us had never heard of the "F" word yet, so no problem there.

But, there was time for that word when we got to high school. Questions in class always led to long discussions about, "Was it still a sin if you said the swear words in your head, or only out loud?" The answer was always the same. "No swearing either way if you want to go to heaven."

When you went to confession, you had to know the difference between a mortal sin and a venial sin, which is a lesser sin. You don't want to mess around with a mortal sin, because then you know you will be damned to eternal suffering and go straight into the fires of hell when you die. That knowledge came with a heavy burden of guilt and caused many whispers around the playground discussing just how bad certain sins may be. Oh, and don't forget to tell the priest in the confessional booth how many times you said the bad words or did the sinful things, I'm just sayin'.

The good thing about confession was that you would be forgiven for all your sins if you did penance which was usually the same for me each time. Five "Hail Mary's" and an "Our Father" or two. Those prayers would be said at a frantic pace kneeling in a pew near the front of the church as far away from everybody else as possible.

Starting with a normal "Hail Mary full of grace, the Lord is with thee," and increasing speed until concluding with, "prayforussinnersnowandatthehourofourdeathamen." Needless to say, in time I was able to increase my speed so well that my sins were removed in really record time.

I guess I have to say I wasn't much of a sinner. I never told lies until I started sneaking off to the roller skating rink in high school, and that was what I considered a sin of omission—I just forgot to tell Mom where I really went—and that wasn't too bad. I did, however, carry with me into my whole adult life a general feeling of guilt as a result of those days that never ceases to amaze me.

The month before graduation we all got a satin ribbon streamer to pin on our uniform to show we were graduating, along with a blue leather, zippered autograph book with Class of 1963 embossed on the cover. In the space listing what my profession will be I wrote, a dancer or a model. For sports I enjoy: skating, dancing, horse riding, and swimming. Swimming? Wait a second, that one wasn't right, I couldn't swim and was terrified of water. Was it a sin to tell that lie? I suppose it was only a yearning to master that sometime down the road (which I never did).

The girls that I had become friends with were the first to sign with flowery notes and poems. Linda, Cheryl, and Jorjean got front pages with something like, "When twilight draws its curtain and pins it with a star, Remember you have a true friend, no matter where you are." Or the ever popular, "2good 2B, 4 got 10."

The boys often signed their name with a sturdy "Good Luck." One brave guy stood out with, "The only rose that has no thorns is the rose that didn't grow" signed by Thomas Z. And this one signed by William W. is a good one to remember, "When you get old and out of shape, remember Sears girdles $2.98."

Then there was the religious themed sayings such as, "If in heaven we don't meet, hand in hand we'll share the heat, and if it gets intensely hot, Pepsi Cola hits the spot." Or this short but sweet one, "Poor poem, poor pen, poor writer, AMEN."

When I managed to make it through eight years of elementary school to a joyous graduation, there was a big family party again, with a graduation cake. Oh, and did I forget to mention, cards and money?

After all that, much to everyone's surprise and

even mine, I chose to go to a Catholic all girls' high school. In those days, we were told only pagans went to public school and if we did, we would be in the presence of sin. So, I took the exam to enroll at Resurrection High School and decided to give it my best shot.

11

High School At Last…
My "Wonder Years," 1963 through 1967

Late in summer before school began, when I went to visit Grandma and tell her all about starting high school, out came the shoebox and I picked out a hanky bordered in purple lace. The bold color purple made me feel brave. No more baby pastels for me. It seemed to signify my beginning adulthood and independence, and that year I became a bit of a rebel.

Resurrection Academy was what it was called when it first opened but quickly morphed into Resurrection High School just before my 1963 class enrolled. A ten-foot tall, black wrought iron fence circled it, with driveway gates that could be locked by a groundskeeper during the day while we were in classes. My four years between 1963 and 1967 were my first taste of a new reality. The school motto was Caritate Et Veritate, which is Latin for Charity and Truth. The truth to me at that time meant that I had to grow up. I could no longer live in the Peter Pan and

Tinkerbell fairytale and refuse to grow up as that story tells. A part of me was ready, but there was a small stubborn part of my soul that dug in and wanted to keep things just the way they were. Going to an all girls Catholic School was a sheltered experience of attempting to strike out and find my own identity but with strictly enforced boundaries.

We received a book full of many rules and a strict schedule. Our freshman and sophomore uniform was navy blue gabardine that changed in junior and senior year to grey wool. The blazer hid any shape under it in a ladylike way. With it a shapeless white cotton blouse with a peter pan collar—whatever that was supposed to mean—was worn. Mini skirts were the new fashion, but our severe a-line skirts had to be worn two inches below the knee, holy cows, indeed!

After the first few days of school, I was one of many girls who rolled up our skirts at the waistband. As we got out of school at 3:00pm, a sudden sausage of fabric would appear at our waistlines showing off long legs running to the bus stop or to awaiting cars. Those of us that were the most daring left them rolled up in school, but when one of the Sisters would see too much knee, you could be asked to kneel on the floor to make sure that the skirt at least touched the floor. Any higher and your reputation would be tarnished forever in their eyes.

We were required to wear ugly grey Hush Puppies shoes that laced up but were soft soled so as not to scratch the new spotless pink marble floors. Every girl had a white chapel veil bordered with nylon lace that we wore once a week for services. It was shoulder length, and we would secure it with bobby pins. We looked like nuns or brides ourselves when we filed into the gym for mass. Oh, the embarrassment of it and how I hated that look!

The Sisters of the Resurrection were an order of nuns established first in Poland. As to the history of my school, the new school was modern bright and beautiful in contrast to the opposite side of the property which was the original school and Provincial Home of the Sisters. That large, dark brick Gothic building was first the high school since 1922, and finally home for Sisters who were old, infirm or dying. It also housed students that were boarding there and postulant nuns studying for the sisterhood. Many of the older nuns still taught if they were able to, and it was always a mystery to me because they seemed so ancient. Rumor had it that some of the Sisters came there directly from Poland sickly and maimed after they survived prison and concentration camps during the Nazi's brutal invasion of Poland in World War II. We would sometimes whisper what we had heard about one or another in sympathy not even fully knowing yet what concentration camps really meant.

They wore long black habits (gowns) with a starched white bib and a headpiece with a veil covering their hair. They wore black leather, old lady style, lace-up shoes that were silent when they walked, allowing them to sneak up on unsuspecting rule breakers. There were a couple of sisters that had a slight squeak in the sole in her shoe and we could always tell when she was coming. They each had a large rosary at their waist made of wooden beads that would clack occasionally when they broke into a hurry instead of floating mode.

My experience with nuns was that I tried to stay just below their radar. I wasn't a very good student, and my parents left it to me to get good grades, barely ever asking about school. In later years, I realized that my mother never went to high school because she had to work to help the family. My father started high school, but never graduated because of the same thing. I think they were both a little afraid of the whole higher educational process and left it to me and the nuns to figure it out. Finally, after my first two years of summer school at Taft High School, I hunkered down and added studying to my social energies to avoid further embarrassment.

I did have a couple of favorite nuns. One in particular was Sister Thomas Aquinas who was my homeroom teacher, Room 109, and she was also my English teacher who loved my writing and coaxed into me a confidence for the first time in my life to keep writing. We called her Sister Tom. She was such a great role model, and our group bonded and worked together like a respectful and loving family. In her room, we laughed, teased, and helped each other. I feel blessed that she came into my life and I will never forget her. Those years were full of laughter, friendships and pranks. I remember the main entrance lobby of the school had a life size statue of the Virgin Mary. A couple of the daring, funny girls were always planting things in her outstretched hands such as cigarettes, food and trinkets. Once someone planted a condom, which some of the girls had never heard of yet. The nuns would announce over the PA system for the ones responsible to report to the principal's office because "We know who you are!"

Adjusting to life in high school was a challenge for me right from the beginning. There were many memorable moments of forgetting where my locker was or even worse, forgetting the locker combination. Numbers were never my strong suit, so remembering locker combinations and room numbers struck fear in my heart. Even in later years, I still had nightmares about that. To balance my insecurities, I had my music, as always, and that was a huge part of my life. I started collecting 45-rpm records and built up quite a collection.

Then one day, my trusty transistor radio started playing new music from an obscure British group called The Beatles. That was when I really began to sit up and take notice. "I Want To Hold Your Hand" and "She Loves You" were the next 45 rpm records that I bought, and I played them over and over and over. Their music really spoke to me and all of the girls at school started talking about that *new* group from England. At the end of a boring winter, when they appeared on The Ed Sullivan show in 1964, I talked my whole family into watching together. I became hooked for years after those adorable and talented Beatles blew into our lives!

If I was asked to remember one day that stood out in my high school years, I would have to recollect the one day I will never forget. That autumn of freshman year, we were to have our first big assembly in the theater. All of the students were gathered in the school lobby ready to file into the theater. It was November 22, 1963, and we would be singing special patriotic songs in honor of President Lincoln and the anniversary of his Gettysburg Address speech he gave on November 19th, 1863. We had been practicing songs about Illinois where he was born and other patriotic songs.

As we stood ready to file into the theater, an announcement came over the intercom that President John F. Kennedy had just been shot in Dallas, Texas. You could hear a subtle gasp in unison as we were asked to all pray for our dear president. Tears sprang to our eyes as we went to take our seats. Before we began, Sister Lydia Mary, our principal, stood on the stage and in a tearful voice, relayed that she had just heard that he had died of his wounds. We all said prayers in unison for him and his family. Then we were asked to sing our little concert not only in the honor of President Lincoln, but of another great president in our history, John Fitzgerald Kennedy and to remember him in our hearts. What a difficult task it was for me and for others around me. Singing with a lump in our throats, tears in our eyes and hearts breaking in sympathy for the man, who seemed so young and invincible, and his family. That day, and the days immediately following through his televised funeral, remained in my memory for the rest of my life.

The older I get, I realize how precious those memories are of the years I started to grow into myself. I loved art classes, until I knocked over a purple wax sculpture of Jesus' hand and broke it before an important Art Exhibit. Sister Gabrielle was not happy to say the least and for two days, I broke into a cold sweat thinking there might be a lynching every time I passed that hall. But, even that didn't deter me from my lifelong interest in art.

As for life lessons I learned through those years, most of them were how to understand and respect those around me and to fully appreciate my life. I began to see the example that the nuns were trying to set for us, they were intelligent, strong women who tried to teach us that in life we must cultivate order and that empowerment was actually in each of us. The sad part is that I didn't fully understand those lessons until many years later, but when it came, it was loud and clear like a light in a closet had just turned on in the dark. I finally began to appreciate the efforts of those Sisters like a delayed reaction.

I must confess that during those years, I began to question the religion that I was brought up in. Being a Catholic who was told from day one, that my religion was the one and only true religion, planted seeds of doubt in me as I started to learn about other religions. It was the 60s, and I started to see the world as a very diverse place to live in, mixed with so many varied races and religions. I pushed hard against my taught beliefs and began to question some of them. I believed in some of the teachings, but not all of them. It was then that I realized that I was a very "spiritual" person but not necessarily a "religious" one. I still struggled with feelings of guilt for doubting my faith, but I vowed to continue to learn about all religions and beliefs going forward and practice not to judge them.

The most important gift I received at Res— what we called our school in abbreviated form—was the friendship of wonderful girls who grew up to be wonderful women. They all inspired me. I can still see their faces and hear our laughter. There were the usual Winter Formals, Ring Dance, and Senior Prom, but at the end of junior year, some of the girls and I decided to have one big party celebrating summer vacation. We wanted to have it in my backyard because there was more than enough space. We invited everyone we knew.

Sue had a jukebox in her basement, so Heather, Janis, and I borrowed Heather's parents station wagon and begged our dads to help stuff that huge jukebox into the back of her station wagon to get it over to our house. We begged and borrowed all the latest top 45's to load the music, and had our little party on a warm summer night. Little did we know how word would get around, and it turned out to be well over 100 crazy, dancing high school and college students (compliments of older brothers and boyfriends). My poor mom and dad kept watch from the living room in front of the house, pointing out the one single bathroom when needed. Dad commented after the party was over, "They all seemed like good kids," much to my amazement and relief. Once again our backyard of the little house on Argyle Street, complete with apple orchard, was put to good use making memories.

I had a stuffed doll that I named Thaddeusz that was pretty ugly, but we girls were so silly, we took him around everywhere like he was our baby brother. The guys thought we were very strange, but we always got a lot of laughs out of that fur covered, baby-sized, orange haired little guy. Sometimes, we would put funny little baby clothes on him or a hat. We were so goofy and could laugh for hours until we choked about all of our nonsense.

I had the best friends any girl could wish for. At the top of the list was Janis who had her driver's license first and drove me everywhere. We became friends when we would meet at The Hub roller skating rink, and we would skate to the big pipe organ music to our hearts delight and flirt with those "older guys." That place was my main destination two or three times a week if I could talk my parents into it. Those were the days of my first rebellion, for I would sneak there at least one night a week. I loved skating to All Skate and Ladies Only and if I got asked to do a waltz, I was in seventh heaven as the mirrored spotlight globe twinkled through the song. Moon River still plays in my memory reminding me of those nights. Janis and I started skating in sixth grade until around sophomore year when new friends began to pull us both away from The Hub.

Janis and I were only twelve and thirteen at the time we met there, but somehow we had such a common bond that it was inevitable we would be friends our entire lives. And it is to our good fortune that we always have been. Such loyalty from her was awesome, and she inspired me in so many ways because I didn't have the courage for many things. I didn't even get my drivers license until after I graduated from high school at the age of eighteen. And of course there was Darlene (Dar), the only Italian in our group. She was the most beautiful girl who had a steady boyfriend (John, AKA Johnny B. Good). Those two were such a stable couple in spite of their tender ages. They literally adopted us single girls and chaperoned us on all of our adventures. John kept an eye on us and didn't let his friends take advantage of us. He treated us as if we were Darlene's sisters. Sometimes when we got too out of control with our shenanigans, we would get the stink eye from him and the silent treatment. We tried to avoid that because we all loved him, even then.

We went to sock hops in various Catholic high

school gymnasiums. Live bands played, and everyone respectfully left shoes at the door so as not to ruin or dirty the wooden gym floors. We went to Oriel Park every Friday night for basketball games where John and his team of friends, Jim, Tom, Roger and the guy's put just the right amount of spice into our otherwise boring lives. It was hard to meet guys when you went to an all girls' school. Afterwards, we would all caravan to Esposito's Italian Restaurant in Niles and have pizza and cherry Cokes. George (Georgeanne)— my sweet Polish buddy whose last name started with a W like mine, and didn't have an ski at the end, also like me—was the hilarious and always laughing buxom blond. She always had an open house for us, and her mom and dad allowed many sleep over's and parties there. She loved *everyone* without reservation, and everyone loved her right back. When she passed away so suddenly a couple of years after graduation, the shock sent a blast of separation through our group that none of us ever really got over.

"Dear George, we haven't forgotten you. Wait a bit longer and our gang will be back together again soon, and we'll pick up right where we left off."

My most vivid memory was the big snowstorm of January 26, 1967. It was our senior year and the countdown had already begun toward prom and graduation day. Two days before the snow started, it was a balmy 65 degrees and we thought that we may have an early spring. Then two days later, school let out at 1PM because snow was accumulating so fast the bus lines had already closed, and cars were stuck along closed roads. Within an hour, there was no vehicle traffic and after we all walked miles to our various homes from school, Janis and I again walked from our homes all the way back up Milwaukee Avenue to George's house in Niles to spend the night with Carol, and Darlene.

The beauty of that night still remains in my mind. It was total silence on the streets and a heavy layer of white snow muffled all human sounds. Our only companion was Mother Nature and big flakes of snow coming down steadily on us as we trudged through the center of each street to our destination five miles away. It didn't seem like a long walk because we bundled up, and we loved the adventure of the idea. When the snow finally stopped, the next day the sun broke out shining on a fairyland record of twenty-three inches of snow, not even counting the drifts.

We always would hang out in George's basement and listen to records. Our favorites were the Mamas and Papas ("California Dreaming", and "Dedicated to The One I Love"); the Association

("Windy" and "Cherish"), and anything by the Beatles (there were so many of their hits). We sang songs of The Four Seasons together in harmony and danced to songs by The Temptations, Buckinghams and The Young Rascals.

The guys in our group were our dates for dances, and we spent almost every weekend together just hanging out. They were all like big brothers to us. Tom, Jim, Ron and a few of their other friends gave us girls our first taste of dating manners of which we really had none. There were two favorite's named Tom. One of them, Tom K., was our resident funny guy. He had a convertible, and we would all pile in to go to the May Day Polish Band celebrations at Polonia Grove. Even though it was May, temperatures were still bone chillingly cold and windy. That year, all of us girls had gotten a short Sassoon haircut in honor of the biggest fashion trend, those fabulous British Beatles. We dressed in our best skin-tight corduroy jeans and our new, white leather, beaded, fringed moccasins. It was not "cool" to wear socks with them, so we braved the wet slush and went without. The rest of the year, we all wore leather penny loafers with knee socks, but when the first glorious days of spring thaw came, out came those moccasins.

Off we would go to any place with music or pizza usually with Tom K. I forgot to mention that he played drums and would cart them around in the trunk of his car and play along to our favorite 45 rpm records to add a little excitement to our goofy gatherings, so I guess you could say with a grin, we had our own band. John played the accordion and would break into an occasional polka just to get a group groan. At the time, I didn't understand the importance that those days would play in my life. The constant giggles and laughter we shared still echo in my memory. Those years were the frosting on the cake of our lives.

If you have been blessed with a fairly trouble free youth as I was, surrounded by friends and family, that "magic" can never be duplicated. It is like trying to hang on to the glittering tail of a comet. We all must grow up and can't stop the clock for that's what life is all about, the minutes and seconds just keep ticking away. At that time, I felt like I was finally an adult but in reality, I was still only in the cocoon stage just starting to break out a tiny bit, not knowing that much more time is needed to complete that stage before an adult butterfly emerges. When I look back, I can say that those days were our "glory days." We were so blessed to have shared them together.

My Senior Year yearbook quote: "I want to live every day of my life as if it were my last." Now I ask you, What kind of young high school teenager writes something so serious? Well, that is a part of me, I guess. I have always been serious about making each day count for something. I never really accomplished anything of note in my life that would appear in the Times newspaper. Just between you and me, don't publish this memoir anywhere? OK? My writings over the years have been heartfelt, occasionally teary, sometimes humorous, long-winded, and sometimes too private to share, but I always spoke and wrote how I feel and about who I am, so I guess it's nothing new to the people who know me.

If I'm writing, whether a letter or card, I add way too many exclamation points and dots…I get carried away with punctuation to add drama. Yep, that's me. "Drama Queen." And, I can still envision each "Act" of my life as if I am seeing it performed on a stage. I'm not sure where the Intermission is, or am I living it now? I have begun to wonder where and when the Final Act or Finale will be. But when that curtain goes down, and I take that final bow along with all of my beloved cast members, I know I will be filled with satisfaction and contentment for a role well played the best that I knew how.

12

Kathie And Glenn
1968 through 1970

I met Glenn Robert Staniec in 1968 when I was 18 years old, and I was committed to him right from the start. I can't explain how that can happen, serendipity, love at first sight, whatever defines that. It's still a mystery to me. We met at a party in the old neighborhood of Chicago quite a ways from my suburban home. My friend Carol drove, and Judy and I didn't even know where we were. No GPS systems or computers to check an address. We had only a huge paper map to try our best at reading in the dark with a dim map light overhead. We finally found the party address and went down in the basement of a friend of a friend's house, but Carol already had enough and said she was leaving. We thought she was kidding and ignored her because we were starting to have fun and an hour later, we looked for her and found out she did leave us. Stranded! Judy and I panicked and knew we couldn't call our fathers to pick us up. They would be furious that we went to a party in the old neighborhood in the city 20 miles away.

Some of the guys we knew told us to talk to the guy who threw the party. Glenn was a friend of theirs and they said, "He's a really nice guy and he might take you home." Well we found Glenn, introduced ourselves, and explained our situation, and he did take us home. He was like a knight in shining armor and even got us home by curfew at midnight. He was so handsome to my eyes. Until then, I had only dated short guys. Glenn was 6'2" tall, with an athletic build, striking blue eyes, and wavy brown hair. He had a great smile and even teeth that looked like Chicklets Gum. To me, he was a dream come true. He asked for my phone number and I waited every day for a call from him.

When he finally did call after two weeks, we talked on the phone for hours. After our first date it was only a short time before we became "exclusive."

He gave me his Lane Tech High School ring that I wore with angora yarn wrapped around the back of it because it was so big. He was nine months older than me, and a junior at University of Illinois, downtown Chicago. I was working at Allstate Insurance Company at the time. And by the end of that year, we started to look at engagement rings any time we walked past a jewelry store. I couldn't help myself and started buying Brides magazines and hid them from my Mom. I didn't want her to start asking questions yet.

One day, Glenn asked my dad if it was OK to ask me to marry him and surprisingly, Daddy gave his approval. Glenn never officially proposed, because he was sort of shy about that but it was fine with me that we just began to talk about our wedding as if we had been planning it forever. I just never envisioned that would ever happen for me. Then Daddy sent Glenn and me to a jeweler that he said, "Would give us a good deal." Freddie da Jeweler, was what all the neighborhood people called him.

We went to the address on Ashland Avenue, in the old neighborhood and found a "door" with the numbers on it. No windows or sign. When we opened the door, there was a little wooden counter in a space about 4 feet by 4 feet with a little man sitting behind it that looked like a tiny garden gnome. He was not a cute gnome, just shriveled and scary. We said, "Casey sent us." And he asked, "What kinda ring ya lookin' for?" Just then, the door to the street behind us opened and the mailman had to come in to deliver the mail. We had to go out the door and wait on the sidewalk so the mailman could come in to deliver. Then, we went back in to talk to Freddy. He sent us to the Merchandise Mart Jewelry floors to take a look, and we had my dream ring sent to him to finish. It was a solitaire diamond and the mounting was yellow gold with a naked lady holding up a cup that the diamond rested in. There were vines and a flower bud wrapped around the dainty vintage setting. I loved the vintage look and have admired that style my whole life. It was a setting that no one would ever have but me.

When I got the ring and began to wear it, everyone politely looked at it and said, "Is it a real engagement ring?" And I told everyone that I wanted something completely different and original, and it sure was. I was so happy, and Glenn, the dear guy, never criticized me. He was happy if I was happy. I have always had that darn creative streak running through me and used every opportunity to express it.

Let me give you a little background about what drew Kathie and Glenn to each other. In the beginning, like all romances, chemistry plays a large part in it and who can explain that? Certainly, I cannot answer that. Similar background was a prime piece of the puzzle. Both sets of parents were raised in the depression always lacking in financial stability. Both of our dads worked constantly. Right out of elementary school all four of our parents quit school to work and help support their families.

On the flip side, both mothers were stay at home mothers when they married and had children.

Glenn's mother didn't know how to drive a car, and his father worked nights as a chef and that left Glenn on his own a lot to get to baseball games and practices by bus. Glenn's parents were a loving duo, and his mother and dad were much like mine. We both had one sister who was three years younger. His family and mine were all close to cousins, aunts, and uncles and we loved them all.

Both families had lots of parties, and everyone always drank too much alcohol and smoked too many cigarettes. Arguing constantly was as much a way of life as was laughing. Sunny and Casey, and Blondie and Stony as they were called, each came of age and married during World War II, and our dads were military. Stony was in the Navy and stationed on a ship at sea as a cook and my father, Casey, was stationed in the states in the Army Air Force and was a gunnery instructor.

As soon as Glenn and I turned fifteen, we both got part time jobs after school and weekends. Glenn worked at the Lajoya grocery store a few blocks from his house stocking shelves and working the deli meat counter. I worked at Turnstyle, a small department store (like Target) in the lingerie department, folding bras and granny panties into divided tables almost my whole shift.

As for me, I'm not used to compliments and

certainly never got much of that growing up. I was *expected* to do well and be good, but I was never questioned about how I was doing or was that ever discussed. If I was having any trouble with anything, I kept it to myself and that's how Glenn was raised as well. Our parents came from a generation in which compliments were not given out freely. We didn't have a very secure sense of self-confidence, and tooting our own horn was not something we were comfortable with.

We both attended Catholic elementary schools and had an underlying sense of guilt peppered with fear of "sin" though we never discussed that. We seemed to always just live up to the status quo and keep our heads above water in our families.

I was in awe of Glenn's work ethic and drive. Where I did not excel at my studies or have much educational interest at the time, Glenn was much stronger and thankfully, I know that his parents did play a role in that. He finished College with a Bachelor's Degree in Business Management at University of Illinois while working full time to pay his own way. He was paying for his own car payments and insurance as well. I don't know how he still had money to take me out to movies downtown and out to eat at nice restaurants. He would drop his Dad off for work at his night shift and pick him up in the middle of the night to bring him home and drove his sister and mom to any place they needed to go. That was extreme devotion.

He was still going to school and working nights, and dropping off and picking up his family, until he moved out of his house to marry me, and I could see he was exceptionally hard working and determined to succeed. I was so proud of him for all of his accomplishments, and he never complained to me of being tired. A truly amazing guy!

Once we were engaged, I started searching in the newspapers for "Apartments for Rent." I had always wanted to live by Lake Michigan and kind of wanted to be far enough from my family to stretch my wings, and I'm sure he felt the same. We went each weekend to look at apartments and found the *one* meant for us. The Jarvis Street Apartments were in an old brick building. We signed the papers and looked out the third floor window over the courtyard, feeling the pride of finally doing something permanent that was ours together.

It was a pretty building with flowers in the courtyard in spring and summer, tall ceilings and textured stucco walls inside. Beautiful hardwood floors and radiators were both a new thing for me. We couldn't wait to move in.

First things first, ours was the first big wedding

for each of our families. Glenn and I each had a younger sister, and our families put an incredible focus on the "Big Event." We chose "The Lido" a banquet hall on Milwaukee Avenue. Both families split half of reception costs and gosh, were we grateful.

Our parents, when they married, never had a reception of their own, so they wanted to have all of their friends and family there. I know there were some days that they were disappointed in our choices, but we all weathered through and managed to still make it. We had a Polish/Italian family style sit down dinner where bowls and plates of food were passed around each table family style.

We found a five-piece band that played great music through Janis's cousin Linda and booked them. God bless my romantic, childish heart for I wanted everything I ever imagined my wedding could be.

The list of songs was long including songs like "Proud Mary," and current dance hits. We really wanted two of our favorites "Midnight in Moscow" and "Stranger on the Shore" to be played, which are both heavy on the trumpet. The night of the wedding, their trumpet player had a cold sore on his lip and said he probably couldn't do those songs with solo parts, but when he saw the crestfallen looks on our faces, he played them anyway. We were so impressed with his gift of pushing through his pain just for us. Those songs have always remained favorites of ours even years later.

The styles in 1970 were definitely flower power, hippy with flowers in the hair, and simple gowns. But I envisioned myself as a Russian princess like in the movie Dr. Zhivago. I was also in love with the romanticism of Romeo and Juliet, so I went shopping for a wedding dress a full year before and found a beaded headdress and gown at the clearance sale that Mom and Dad could afford. It was a style not like any styles of that time, but I fell in love with it in a moment. I was waiting for a rebellion, but Glenn and his groomsmen, looked at the ruffled raspberry pink shirts I picked for them to wear with the tuxedos and they ordered them! I remember the day Glenn told his buddies about the shirts, and each of them looked at him with eyes popped wide open in shock, but to their credit, they laughed and didn't make any crude comments in public. I think they saved them for when they were alone with Glenn to razz him about the pink ruffled shirts. The bridesmaid's dresses were an unusual violet color with headdresses and a veil trailing down the back like they wore in Romeo and Juliet, complete with a train and gold braid trim. I'm sure they all went along with me while rolling their eyes, but let me have my way for fear of the wrath of

"Bridezilla." I was living in wedding heaven with all the planning.

13

The Wedding And The Newlyweds

Saying "I Do"

On November 21, 1970, our day finally came.
We had a candlelight Wedding Mass at my
neighborhood church, St. Monica. Glenn's talented
cousins played guitars and sang so beautifully the folk
music that we chose. That was another new thing at
that time. Traditionally, organ music was the way to
go, but I walked down the aisle to "A Time For Us"
from Romeo and Juliet and the much-loved song from
West Side Story, "One Hand One Heart." Then a Peter
Paul and Mary favorite, "The Song Is Love," sung in
such beautiful harmony by Glenn's cousins that it was
more like a performance on a stage. Standing in front
of Father Calloran, from Glenn's parish and a church
full of family and friends petrified both of us, and we
could barely speak to say our vows. I was so nervous
that my hands and knees were shaking, and I kept
saying to myself as the smell of incense wafting
through the church was starting to make me dizzy.

"Don't faint in front of all these people, like Patty in second grade." Well we made it, and we almost ran back down the church aisle to exit. Just as we were walking out the doors of the church, big snowflakes drifted down adding the last romantic touch to a picture perfect wedding. At the reception, we danced our first dance together to " I'll Be Loving You, Always," by Frank Sinatra. Then later came the Polish custom of everyone dancing in a circle and passing my shoe around while people put money in it. My Maid of Honor, my sister Janice, placed a satin and lace apron around my waist with six or seven small plastic, naked babies sewn around the hem. I guess that was to signify how many babies I was destined to have. No Thank You!

Finally, we did the garter and bouquet toss, and Mr. and Mrs. Glenn Staniec left the reception to head to the Conrad Hilton Hotel downtown. We sure made a statement as we drove into valet parking with our hubcaps full of rocks making a huge racket. Glenn's friends and cousins had also placed streamers and a Just Married Sign on the back of the car and filled the interior with helium balloons. Strangely, I felt a little like Alice in Wonderland falling down the rabbit hole.

We were both so embarrassed, but went along with a grin for the full wedding experience. We spent the night in our room opening envelopes and counting our money from the moneybag, and Glenn was afraid that someone might rob us. That was the extent of our *honeymoon*. Glenn had only been on one trip to Florida with friends in college. I never traveled except a daring trip to Miami for spring break in high school with my best friend Janis and one long weekend to a college in Iowa for Winterfest with my same trusty friend who always thought I needed to "get a life." As a couple, we were both so naive and even going to a hotel for one night was a challenge for us, so we were in a rush to get to our new little comfort zone on Jarvis Street.

On the day after our wedding, moving in together for the first time was something that I never thought would be so monumental. We thought of everything and had our apartment all furnished and ready to move in after months of work. Why didn't anyone tell us how long it can take to adapt to actually living with a stranger or how much work it takes. Our parents never shared or expressed any personal feelings or advice because they didn't do that in those days. A new chapter in our life together had begun. Neither Glenn nor I had ever done housework or cooked or done repairs.

Back in our new "Home Sweet Home," we had to learn so many new things such as how to light the really old gas stove. You had to light the pilot under each burner or in the oven to cook every time. I was terrified of the whoosh each time the match met with gas. I was sure I would blow the place up. I grew up with an electric stove at Mom's and never learned to cook or bake. High School cooking class was a variety of cakes and appetizers that I never paid attention to except to pass the grade.

Like every girl at Resurrection, we bought a Lane cedar hope chest and dishes at a school fundraiser along with a full set of beautiful shining aluminum pots. My new cooking efforts burned lots of food on the bottoms, and my new sister-in-law Linda had to tell me to scrub it with a Brillo Pad to clean them when we had her over for dinner, and she saw the sorry condition they were in. Stoneware dishes were the new thing and heavy as a ton of bricks, also they were easy to chip when all loaded in the sink to wash at the same time. The presentation at school had assured us that we would surely be brides well equipped for married life with these purchases. I picked out the hope chest that looked like a pirate chest, and my romantic nature wouldn't be swayed away from it. It sat in my bedroom at Mom's until we carried everything up those three long flights of stairs to start our days of wedded bliss.

At the front of our building was Jarvis Street Beach. A sweet pocket sized beach a few steps from our door. That first summer, we loved the beach people and children playing in the sand. It was a time of suntan lotion, sunburn and beach blankets full of sand but every moment we had we enjoyed it, for summer in Chicago is so short. During winter, the weather was so harsh along Sheridan road with wind and ice off lake Michigan swooping around our building. The snow plows had no place to push the snow because our street was a dead end at the beach, so it was usually very icy, and we parked where we could a few blocks away and walked home. We had one car, Glenn's car, and I would walk to the elevated station each day and take the train to the street where a bus would pick up the girls who worked at Allstate Insurance Company in Skokie.

Coming home, there was a tiny grocery store and butcher just under the "El" exit where I would pick up two pork chops or two chicken breasts for our dinner each night. I can remember being so shy the first time about asking the butcher for the meat over the tall glass meat display. I had only seen prepackaged meats in our local grocery store before, so I stood to the side and watched other women order their meats. The first time I stood there, I went home without any until I could get the courage to be bold enough to call out the order loud enough so they could hear me.

That first winter, the waves hit so hard against the sea wall on the side of the building that the water in the toilet would sway back and forth from the vibrations. When we had guests over, Glenn would show them the toilet water moving and tell that story each time with pride as if it was our personal lake and our waves. We could hear the sound of waves as we left the house, and the booming sound was comforting after we got used to it. Watching the waves filled with ice chips churning back and forth was Mother Nature's gift because it formed ice sculptures in corners of the yard along the beach that changed and grew as winter progressed.

That was the year that we changed and grew into a married couple with just as much drama as the location we lived in, and it wasn't easy. Whoever coined the phrase "Wedded Bliss" wasn't being totally realistic. We bickered and said things that were hurtful, while struggling to get on the same page. Both of us were used to having our mothers or dads take care of everything for us and when Glenn expected me to have his laundry sparkly clean, ironed, and ready to wear like his mother did for him so easily, we reached a brick wall. I worked every day too and got home at the same time each day as he did. OK, Maybe I got home an hour or two earlier, but still, I didn't even iron my own clothes. I only bought clothes that were wrinkle free, so I didn't have to do it. If a skirt got a little too rumpled, I would leave it under a sofa cushion to press out the dents in the fabric. It took all of my energy to plan, shop for and cook a dinner. Cleaning toilets, sinks, and the tub was another weekly chore I detested and got in the habit of making excuses not to. We finally agreed to take turns. Problem solved!

One day after we had been married for two months, I realized that I our laundry baskets were full to overflowing and our underwear drawers were empty. I looked at Glenn and said, "What do we do now?" We could take it all to my mother's house and have a laundry day, but I didn't want her to laugh at me. With her one washer and dryer, it would probably take us more than one day. He said that he guessed we probably could go to the neighborhood laundry. Neither of us had ever used ours at home. We didn't even realize that there were a couple of machines in the dark dingy basement of our building. So, we loaded every basket and box we had into the car with our stuff and found the closest Laundromat. I think we filled eight machines in a row that first day and discussed in whispers, with embarrassment, how to start the machines and add detergent. As we tried to figure out the mechanics of sorting laundry, it took us a while to separate darks from lights. When Glenn held up a couple pairs of my pastel bikini panties in the air and called over to my far end of the machines, "Where do you want me to put these shorts?" I noticed a few women nearby smile and look away at my embarrassment. I just stepped over and grabbed them and muttered, "Put them where your shorts are, and they're panties, not shorts." It took us almost that whole first year to come to an agreement on ways to share responsibilities and divide household chores. We did ultimately survive and learned many lessons along the way, and we did it a little bit at a time. On the fun side, we bought our first piece of antique furniture, a six foot long, solid wood buffet that must have weighed over one hundred pounds and hauled it up three flights of stairs with lots of fuming and fussing and, we refinished it ourselves. Glenn installed our first Tiffany style light fixture above the dining room table that we saw at our favorite pizza place. We asked the owner where he got it and he ordered it for us, and we continued to "cozy" up our little nest.

Our first Christmas, we borrowed her old fake tree from Mom. It was our first Christmas tree together that started our favorite tradition of all. It went right in front of the big glass windows facing the courtyard, and we would go down the three flights of stairs to stand outside in the cold and snowflakes to look up at our little lighted tree shining above. The tree had artificial green branches color-coded that took all day to set up because nothing seemed to fit right. We got it as a cast off because the popular tree of the season was still a silver metal revolving trees with an electric colored wheel shining from below in red, green, blue and gold glass to shine on the bright glittering silver. In contrast, our new gold silk covered Styrofoam ornaments and gold garland and colored mini lights seemed like the most beautiful to us.

Together, we made a pretty good team. I thought up decorating projects way back then, and Glenn figured out how to accomplish them. We learned to do all sorts of things together. Painting walls, repairs, gluing fabric on walls, and a myriad of other creative things. We bought two twin Schwinn bikes to travel down the lakeshore paths from a friend. A few months later we found out that they were stolen bikes and from then on, we were afraid the police would come and get us and I for one, always kept a lookout for them often losing my balance in a panic when I would see a police car. I was more concerned to know, was it still a sin if you didn't know the bikes were stolen when you got them? The next summer, our bikes were stolen, and I was almost relieved. My answer to that was, "What goes around, comes around," and that is the end of that story.

The familiarity of being married became easier with time. I teasingly nicknamed Glenn "Spanky" after the spunky leader of the *Our Gang Comedies*. In an endearing way, I was his Darla, but that name died early over the years. In my estimation, Darla was a little too confident, and I would not have confidence like that for so many more years. Besides, I already had so many names and of all the Our Gang members, I was more of a Farina.

At the end of that year, we got a teeny tiny little Miniature Schnauzer puppy, and I hid him in a big purse to take him in and out to visit our folks. Pets were not allowed in our apartment building, but we were planning to move in the coming months. We named him Jarvis after the street of our first apartment.

14

Homeowners

The Home Depot Diaries

For pastime, we would take long drives on weekends to see other suburbs. We looked at open houses and model homes and discussed our dream home. On a winter day in the middle of a snowstorm, we drove out to Elk Grove Village to check out an ad we had seen in the newspaper. Then a week later, we bought our first home and planned our move to 700 B Bordeaux Court in the far western suburbs. We chose it from a model and it would be finished the following spring. We loved our little two-bedroom townhome. It bordered Cosman Lake and the forest preserve and we rode our new bikes around the lake on weekends with Jarvis in a basket on my bike.

I'll never forget my first day at work at a new job in Elk Grove. The adjoining industrial area was all brand new as were the homes around it. The streets were newly tarred and clean. I interviewed for an office job on a hot Friday and was told I could start on the following Monday. Now, picture the dirty slushy winters in the Chicago area. The white beauty of the fresh snow would turn black and ugly, and chunks of frozen slush would drop off the parked cars as days wore on. Well, we moved into our brand new house with an electric garage door opener, and the concrete in the garage was spotless and clean. I thought we should keep it that way, and so Glenn and I went to KMart and bought a big 9 x 12 foot gold shag rug in a bag and went home and spread it across the garage floor to keep it clean.

After my interview on Friday, I drove home elated and parked my old Rambler car in the garage. On Monday as I backed out of the garage, my car came to a sudden stop while in reverse. In a panic I thought, "Uh, oh, what's going on with my car? I put in drive and it went up a few inches and came to a sudden jarring stop again. I tried backing up and no luck, so I put it park while it was halfway out of the garage and got out to look. When I had driven home on Friday, I had driven over a freshly tarred road, and it dried over the weekend. The tar stuck my tires to the shag rug, so when I went in reverse and drive a few times the whole rug got pulled up into my wheel wells and was jammed in there. With tears in my eyes and panic in my voice, I called my new boss Mary and told her I would not be into work due to a car problem. She said, "I see by your address you live close to here, so how about I send Horst from the warehouse to come take a look. He can probably fix it."

In misery, I said OK, knowing my new job might depend on it. I sat in the upstairs window and watched as a truck came by, and Horst got out and stared at my car from all sides and with a perplexed look, scratched his head a few times and got back in his truck and drove away. I realized what a mess I was in and called Glenn at work downtown beg him to come home and try to help me get the car going. When he got home, he laughed hysterically and hacked and pried the rug off the tires with garden tools as best as he could, leaving little clumps of gold shag rug still stuck around all four of my tires.

Finally, I gratefully went to work. I parked near the warehouse door and ran in late to start my first day. My new boss Mary smiled and laughed as she greeted me and said Horst came back to tell them of my dilemma, and my story would probably be famous in the history of the company for many years. As I left for home again that first day, all of the warehouse guys were standing at the parking lot door and laughed when they saw me and gave a thumbs up with a couple of other comments about the fuzz on my tires. Thus began my new life in a new house with a new job.

When we wanted to start a family, we moved to our dream home on Crestwood Lane in Bloomingdale. Oddly, we went to see it for the first time on another snow-stormy day as we had found our first little townhouse. A classic U-shaped ranch with four bedrooms, and a family room with a fireplace was a dream come true. Those next years were filled with learning how to mow the grass, plant and nurture flowers, landscape, and practice household repairs. I started to decorate like a demon and wallpapered every room in the house. Glenn and I spent most of our time together sharing household jobs and learning along the way. Needless to say, we spent a lot of time at Home Depot. Those friendly guys with the bright orange aprons saved us ten times over.

15

Notes On Motherhood And Marriage

And some other really serious stuff

It was seven years from our wedding and after starting treatment with a fertility specialist, Dr. Bloodgood (his name suited what a character he was), that we finally had our baby, Ryan. Our lives changed forever. It was instant love in a bundle of blue-eyed baby boy after trying for three years. From that day on, my heart became permanently bonded to this new little life. I finally felt complete and so happy. Each day was a new adventure for me right along with every new little thing Ryan learned. Both sets of our parents, though they were thrilled with the first grandson, were not the babysitting kind. Distance and time never allowed much help from them. What was so fortunate for us was that Ryan was such an easy baby to raise. He liked his schedule and life's routines to be predictable and was most comfortable with no surprises. That's when I finally learned how to master the art of multitasking, and it was a priceless skill I used constantly the rest of my life. Glenn went to work early each day from the train station to downtown and returned home around seven PM for dinner. He missed out on so much of Ryan's early years, but I was the lucky one to stay at home and take care of everything else.

Shortly after, our dog Jarvis became quite sick. He was such a good little dog, and we loved him dearly. He would sit by Ryan and keep guard over him and when Ryan just started to walk, Jarvis would trot by his side in case of a fall. I bought Jarvis little red rubber boots for snow and icy days and some nice sweaters to keep him warm. He developed kidney stones and over the next few years, he had to be taken to the Veterinarian often and be on a special diet until the day he had surgery and passed away. Poor puppy.

Three years after Ryan was born, following another miscarriage and more fertility treatments, finally we were blessed with a second son, Kevin. We felt we were a perfect little family. He was born a big baby just under ten pounds, and his big brown eyes didn't miss one single thing right from the start. From his very first day, I always felt that he was an old soul. Whenever I looked into his eyes, I could see that he was already aware of everything in the world even at his tender age. Kevin had a little bit of a rough start with digestion and for both of us it was throw up time after almost every meal. He finally outgrew it around three months old. Everyone and the doctors had so many ideas and remedies, and we tried everything. Ryan was a sweet little helper and would get the old diaper burp cloths ready right after feeding time. We had a routine going day by day and with that, the years continued to fly by. Meanwhile, every day Glenn went to work, I stayed home and took care of the house and family. All seemed to be going well until a depressing rash of joblessness forced us to make that tough decision to take the offer to move west and the rest of that story is history...

In looking back over those years, my biggest joys were Ryan and Kevin. On the day each boy was born, love came into my life. The best kind of love! Those were the two projects that I threw myself into from the day I first learned I was pregnant and have never stopped yet. Most times, I did a really good job mothering but some days, not so much. I researched books (good old Dr. Spock and others) and surveyed friends and family endlessly about what they felt worked best. I tried all the advice of the pediatrician. I may not have always said the right thing or done just the right thing. Sometimes, I failed with all good intentions, but I really always tried. Other times, I tried too hard, much to the annoyance of my family. But life can be imperfect, and I encountered many bumps in the road. A mother's role in life is a challenge every day in their children's lives. We must teach, nurture, coerce, argue, sometimes criticize, support, reprimand, worry, and sometimes holler and yell. There were many childhood illnesses that scared us to death and funny little things the boys would do to test our patience that were no less memorable. There was Kevin, at three, juggling four eggs in the air and not understanding that when you throw them up they came down and landed on the floor in a messy smash. There was the day ever helpful, Ryan opened a whole new box of Cheerios and all of it ending up on the floor instead of the bowl. Even Jarvis was appalled and stood looking at him with doggie sympathy.

Then there was the day Kevin opened all of his little boxes of raisins and stuck them on the wall in a line all the way around the room. I went in his room later and for a frantic moment, I thought they were bugs. So many of little scraped knees and soothing hurt feelings, and answering "but why, Mommy?" a million times, are part of raising children. We try our best through all sorts of things in our children's lives and sometimes we end up in tears of frustration ourselves and a helpless fear that we haven't done enough or done it right, while we still love them endlessly. I think I have done all of those things. I'm hoping that even when I'm gone they will still hear my voice in their mind, and it will help them through their lives in a positive way.

Now here comes the hardest part of my story. It's the section in my memoir that I most dreaded to write about. I don't even want to separate it by a chapter or a sub-title. I feel as if it should be squished in between all the other of life's passages, and I wasn't sure where to place it. Not even clutching one of Grandma's lace trimmed hankies would give me enough courage to get through this, but I feel I must. I have lain awake in my bed on many sleepless nights trying to decide how to be true to my story without baring my heart and soul and exposing the blackest part of my existence. By hiding it, I would not be truthful to our journey to the dark side. I suddenly feel I need to share it, because in our story, the beauty of coming out to the glorious brightness of day again could not be understood in any other way. Looking back on my marriage, there are many dark areas. They are embarrassing to me even now, but Glenn and I were human after all.

I always kept reminding myself that the other women that I knew best in my life had many difficult times as well, yet they still would start over again each morning. I can only imagine their seemingly hopeless trials because the times would not allow sharing those innermost thoughts in those days. I choose to share some of mine in my memoir because some words here or there may help another person to keep on going. On my better days, I tried hard not to whine or complain when the chips were down, and I occasionally had to vent to let off some of that steam. There is no easy way to explain how the constant tug of fear, anxiety, sadness, and shame can erode even the strongest personality. I realize how many women have loved someone who had an addiction to alcohol or drugs and how difficult that made living. Like all alcoholics and their families, most was left unsaid only to try to hide everything possible from everyone around you. Pretending everything is normal becomes a way of life. It's a lonely road to travel for everyone involved. It was not that I didn't know what drinking too much at a party was likely to end with, but this was another thing altogether.

I didn't realize the full extent of it early on in my marriage. I mistakenly thought that it would be different with Glenn if I tried hard enough to be perfect, and he had me to love and support him. But, I was very wrong. Glenn fell backwards because of his dependency, so I pushed harder to compensate for him. I think in retrospect that I burned out trying too hard, and then actually overcompensated, and that probably was not a help to him. When Glenn and I went to counseling, I finally realized that was a very typical response given the situation we were in. Learning what I did through counseling, I finally got permission not to judge myself so harshly.

AA meetings helped him temporarily, but after years of that roller coaster we knew it was not a solution. I have decided not to go back and drag out the details of what happened through those years or what it was like for me except to use a song as a metaphor. I have always loved stage musicals and during my darkest years, the song "Memories" from the Broadway hit Cats was always lurking in a corner of my mind. Even though I would try to banish it from my mind it kept popping up. After many restless nights, I would wake up just as early light was seeping through my window feeling overwhelmed by hopelessness. I could picture poor, bedraggled Grizabella singing that song under the streetlamp, as the melody would cushion my way to consciousness each day. If I could only print the lyrics of this song, it would explain her hopeless, lonely existence as she lived in the dark shadows of her world. Sweet memories of happier days can bring comfort, but reality comes again with each dawn as it did for me. Clutching at the courage to start over each day is all that remains for us, and that is how my life had become. I felt so helpless, but I knew it was up to me if any change would be the remedy to help Glenn. I couldn't give up. After meeting a new doctor that I found and checking Glenn into an alcoholism treatment center for two months, we finally got that second chance.

I have to attest that it was Glenn who was strong enough to finally banish his demons and I know it was not easy for him. There are some years that I would have loved to skip entirely to avoid the pain and fear that came with them but those years forced us to be so much stronger. The heat of the fire is what makes steel strong. Glenn spoke often of how grateful he was that he had made it through that time. He often referred to it as a miracle that was his alone.

Unfortunately, I know that those bumps in the road that I got over also must have affected my precious boys. It is tremendously difficult as a parent to let our children endure any pain. If I sensed their despair or confusion, I took it on as if it were my own. I often let it silently ruin me, but I still went to battle for my boys like a mother tiger to try to spare them instead. Life in families with alcoholism are a particularly dangerous environment for children. In later years, long after Glenn had stopped drinking, sometimes we could see there was damage that we were not aware of at the time. Like a ticking bomb, families of alcoholics never know when the damage may become known. That I was a party to that, I can only hope and pray that I was good enough and strong enough to shelter them from as much as possible.

In looking back over those hardest years, if I were given a chance to start over and choose someone else to marry, I know it would still be Glenn once again. Some things in life are like that. I miss him now as much as I loved him, which is immeasurable. We had a roller coaster ride of a marriage together, but I knew from the first day I met him he was the one. He was a good, kind, faithful friend and husband, father, and Papa and always tried his best.

16

The California Years

Growing pains - Adjusting to a new life

Two months before our move-in date, I flew out
on my first trip to California *alone*, and I had three
days to find a home. My best friend Janis, had just
settled out in Southern California recently herself, and
I had just said a tearful goodbye thinking I might never
see her again. Well, a few months later and an offer of
a job for Glenn prompted a surprise phone call from
me to Janis announcing, "I'm coming." Like a
guardian angel, she picked me up at the airport. She
was living temporarily with her cousin Bob and his
wife Jo who welcomed me with open arms to stay with
them. We all pored over the newspaper, circling
"possibles" while Bob checked the Thomas Guide and
tagged every page for us. Janis drove me around
following "For Rent" signs that whole weekend. It was
like a surreal movie to find a place within three days
and that was nothing short of a miracle. I didn't even
know anything about the neighborhoods or school

districts. All I knew was that I had a really strong feeling that I couldn't question, so I had to put my trust in God and the universe and hope and pray I wasn't making a mistake. I felt that somehow we were guided along to that one place for a reason. Our future depended on me and inside, I had a stomach full of butterflies. Janis always had unlimited confidence that was contagious as always and if not for her, I may not have moved here at all. She still claims it was the best thing I have ever done with my life, and I surely agree. The day before I was scheduled to fly back home we got off the freeway to grab a quick bite at McDonalds and saw open house signs in Rossmoor. I fell in love with the neighborhood at first sight, and a realtor directed us to a sign a few blocks away for Townhome for rent. A few hours later, we met my new landlord who was an old Italian man who rented it to me with only a personal check deposit and one page of a filled out form, saying to me "here's the key, I trust you," and that was all that he needed.

When our cross-country car trip from Chicago to LA finally ended late that August summer evening, we turned the key in the lock and stepped across the threshold to our new life. We unloaded all our bedding and pillows from the car, spreading them out on the floor of the master bedroom together and with deep sighs, fell into exhausted sleep. When we opened our eyes the next morning, the moving truck was there and the sun was shining through the windows welcoming us to sunny Southern California. That day was the first day of the rest of our lives. With our travels across the country to our new home behind us, we each experienced a rapid stage of new growth. We rented that Tanglewood Townhome in Cypress until the house in Bloomingdale sold. Our unit was right along side of a beautiful swimming pool and playground. That was something, as mid-westerners, we seldom had access to. It began to feel like a little bit of heaven. The weather was almost always perfect, and living close to the coast and beaches was a short drive to paradise. Every day was something new.

The downside was that Glenn and I were missing Chicago in a way we never knew we would. We found ourselves drawing comparisons with every new thing we experienced. We were homesick. Chicago and its many suburbs is beautiful and complicated with firmly divided neighborhood lines. As far as friends in our old neighborhood in Bloomingdale, the families were not out often to socialize and neighbors went about their lives pulling in and out of their garages with just a wave, as their garage doors closed again silently behind them. I had met a few other mothers on the street, but when fall and winter came there was not much interaction until summer again. It was my large extended family that I missed and my heart yearned for.

There's a familial closeness in the Midwest that seemed different than out here in easy going Southern California, though it's hard to put a finger on it. If I were to try to explain it, I would use the movie *The Godfather* to help visualize it. Generations of "family" stayed together and spent time sharing every occasion. Lots of close ties with family along with extreme loyalty to each other was the common thread. Dinners, holidays, special occasions, religious ceremonies, and the seemingly endless list were spent by just being together. Uncles, Aunts, cousins and a handful of special friends that became honorary Uncles and Aunts became go-to folks whenever a favor was needed. For instance, "Ya wanna get a deal on a new TV set? Go see my cousin Rocco." Or, "There's gonna be a Holy Innocents picnic with a good Polish band, and I want the whole family to be there." And I can personally attest, what a wonderful tradition that was! Whether Italian, Polish, or any other ethnic group, family's always stuck together unconditionally, the good and the bad of them. Where I grew up, people seemed more hesitant to go beyond the many commitments and demands of their already large family circles. They were a little more wary of strangers. In contrast, the upside of Southern California is that there is a certain casual friendliness, because it seems that everyone is transplanted from somewhere else. Nothing stops those transplants from trying to find connections, grow new roots and eagerly embrace new people and new ideas.

We were so happy to be welcomed by whomever we met and befriended. Countless people would nudge open the doors to friendship knowing they had started just where we were. Many Midwest and Chicago transplants, after seeing a Cubs shirt on the guys or hearing our midwest accent, would immediately extend a greeting and open conversation, even in restaurants and other public places. "Are you from Chicago?" That question became a common greeting of strangers. There is a strong open and liberal current always under the surface that took a little getting used to.

In my estimation, Chicago was moodier, darker, and more complex where California is brighter, lighter and more kicked back. No major public transportation to speak of in California to compare with Chicago. I saw less of a dress code here and was shocked to see ladies wearing house slippers to the grocery store, and men and women alike wore flip flops everywhere most of the year.

There was more of a variety of ethnic areas and restaurants all around with easier access than we had in the Chicago suburbs. In Chicago, there was better pizza, hot dogs, and Italian beef and Polish restaurants. In California, there was better variety of Mexican restaurants along with much more organic and locally grown fresh fruits and vegetables all year long. Avocados, oranges, and lemons even grew in yards, and at Farmers Markets the selections of all fresh produce were unlimited.

While we missed our favorite *Portillo's* for hot dogs and Italian beef, *Lou Malnati's* for pizza or driving up to *Super Dog* for a Whooper Cheesie, we started to find new places to fill in the spaces like *El Torito* and so many other great Mexican restaurants that were primo. *Katella Deli* was like no other restaurant we had back home. The list of restaurants new to us grew so long that we could hardly keep up.

On the sports scene, of course, there were no teams like the Chicago teams for Glenn and the boys. They remained avid fans and loyal to the Cubs, Bears, Bulls and Blackhawks. The Angels here were a novelty as were the Anaheim Ducks, but one thing about Chicago sports fans is that you remain loyal for life, and we all did.

And then, there was Disneyland. For all of the perceived commercial aspect of it, Glenn and I fell in love with it. "The Happiest Place on Earth" was right in our own backyard. On days when we were feeling at odds with our world, we would do one of two things.

One, go to the ocean five miles down the road to watch the waves and the surfers. We could feel the salt air saturate our being with energy. Or two, go the five miles in the opposite direction to Disneyland. What a place to fill our senses with interesting and entertaining sights and sounds. Even people-watching was entertaining to us. It was a magical bonus that put a bandaid over our sore little hearts. We ended up getting annual passes that we never regretted over the years. Glenn and I got ours on our wedding anniversary, so that date was forever connected to our passports. Each year's renewal was our anniversary present to each other. We had them until the year he passed away, and those visits were always a bright memory in our lives and we never tired of it.

The weather in California contrasted sharply with the weather in Chicago. That was the most obvious difference, and we could not get over the pleasant days one after another. I began each day saying to myself, "Another beautiful day in paradise," as I awoke. I loved the sunny, beautiful weather almost each day of the year along with the silky coastal breezes. It was like living in heaven on earth.

The cultural landscape was full of offerings. Southern California was a movie town in general, and many people that we met had some kind of attachment to the film industry. Glenn got two tickets from a man at work for *"A Birthday Tribute to Carol Burnett"* at UCLA Royce Hall. We were living here only 3 months. There were so many celebrities at the cocktail party and dinner, I was totally starstruck in disbelief. They were like real people, and I couldn't believe I lived here to see it. Carol Burnett, Harvey Korman, Tim Conway, Elizabeth Taylor, Julie Andrews, Tom Selleck, and so many others were in attendance. I pretty much was a wall hugger that evening, just watching. Glenn wanted me to circulate and get autographs, but I was speechless and couldn't do it. I even was afraid to go to the ladies room in case I ran into one of the actresses. What a sissy I was! On that day, I think the Hollywood bug bit me.

Even at the children's level, I found it was common to have lots of school performances with singing and dancing and even in fifth and sixth grade, Mrs. Prince and Donna helped the kids put on stage musicals that were absolute showstoppers! It was so amazing to us just how high the bar was set on creativity and talent and those kids met it every time. Many students enrolled in tap, jazz and singing classes in addition to their regular school curriculum. Ryan and Kevin got an introduction to the arts through Orange County Song and Dance Company, and I felt that it would balance out the constant sports. Glenn and I loved to watch the boys perform on stage and were so proud of them. Wherever their group performed, we went along to Disneyland, Knotts Berry Farm, Universal Studios and many other places over a period of five or six years. Ryan and Kevin were multi-talented, and we basked in the glow of each of their successes. They seemed to enjoy performing, but I found out in later years from their grumbling comments, that was not always so. Sometimes, I guess, the parents are the last to know.

As my new California life progressed, I suddenly realized that up to that move, I was still immature and surprisingly naive. Hard reality hit. Even though I was a wife and mother of two little boys, I was still a child myself in many ways. I was my Mommy and Daddy's little girl and was still in their sheltered world, closely tied to my family. I just couldn't understand why I didn't feel like a grown up yet, but being in a new community, I could see differences in the independent women all around me. I was terrified of the freeways and California drivers. The streets went in all directions, and I kept getting lost. Freeways were seven and eight lanes across and frightening to me. My self-confidence, which wasn't good to start with, took a rapid dive.

The move to California began my final metamorphosis. I didn't want myself to feel helpless, and I didn't want to lose my ability to remain intuitive.

I wanted to find new people to befriend in hopes of nurturing new friendships as close as those I had left behind. I knew I had to go slow in that area, for fear of scaring them away, but I was so impatient to make new friends. I had blocked so much of myself in the years that preceded our move and I felt so insecure starting over. Strength can be a complicated package, but I was determined to exercise that. I began to search who I really was and tried to envision what potential I had. The boys adapted more quickly than Glenn and I, as children are prone to do. They liked their new schools, and the school district turned out to be the best of all options for the boys. Once again, I think God was certainly playing a part in yet another miracle.

As it turned out, we all started making friends right away, and I was so grateful for the friendly open people we began to meet. It was easier than I had anticipated and all my worry was for nothing.

"The Musings Of An O.C. Girl"...Once settled in California, we bought our little house in Rossmoor, and it felt like that house had been waiting for us forever. It was a feeling of having arrived at our final destination, and it felt so good. We loved the steady flow of people walking by the house, many times stopping to chat about our garden that became a new

obsession for me. The rhythm of the neighborhood was seasoned with sounds of bikes and skateboards punctuating each day. Even though there were no intense seasonal changes, there was still an ebb and flow of the seasons, gently changing like the tide.

Traffic to and from the schools at each end of our street was timed with the sound of the class bells from September through June marking the beginning, middle, and end of each day. I learned to take a moment to appreciate the sudden peacefulness of the first day of summer vacation. The traffic sounds faded, but that peacefulness was sometimes punctuated by outbursts of children at play echoing from pools nearby. The sound of the tick and spritz of automatic sprinkler systems turning on more often to cool the summer parched plants. The end of August was back to school time and soccer season with practices at every field in the neighborhood. I looked for the subtle change of colors of leaves with only a few trees and shrubs dropping their foliage in December and learned with amazement, that they re-bud again in early March.

One thing that was a familiar tradition was Halloween. In California, there was always big trick-or-treat school events, parades, and neighborhood activities. The weather was perfect for the deluge of costumed children going door to door. Back in the

Midwest, the weather seldom cooperated, and the traditions there were more limited with costumes covered by winter coats as only the bravest went out in cold and rain.

"Absence makes the heart grow fonder"...Missing people became a new reality to deal with. I really missed my Sister Janice and friends from high school. I began to reach out with occasional letters and phone calls to those who remained important to me. I felt closer to them the longer that we lived so far away, which is difficult for me to understand. Judy, who had married Jim, another Lane Tech graduate that Glenn knew of from his high school baseball days, was someone who I tried to keep in regular touch with. She was with me the night I met Glenn. As the years kept flowing by, we didn't touch base very often but somehow in later years, we once again became closer. What a mystery, but an important ingredient in the recipe of my life.

Darlene also became a constant thought in my mind as if a part of me was still there with her almost every day. Strangely, I often wonder what the loveable curmudgeon, John (her husband) would say to me if I were up to any mischief. Mischief is my middle name, and I'm not too old that I can't enjoy a little every now and then. Another friend from High School, Cathy was one of the girls who I tried to keep in touch with after we both married and had children. I knew her husband Gary from when they were first dating in high school, and they were the first of my friends who made a big move out of state from Chicago and started over. They moved to Georgia and became Southerners forever more. I wondered, at the time, how hard that must have been and couldn't understand why they would move so far away. I never even dreamed that I would be next to go.

I miss those girls and think of them often and when we get to talk, we catch up as if I saw them just yesterday. As for my cousins, even though I think of them often, aside from Sandy and Larry who were closest to me in age, the distance and different stages of lives have split us farther apart. Larry now lives in San Diego and sadly, my cousin Sandy has passed away as almost all of the Happel sisters have as well. My cousins Karen and Roxanne are still always on my mind as well as all of the other cousins who live spread out all over. The last remaining Happel sister, sweet Auntie Nancy (no longer little Pisspot) and her family have all moved to Wisconsin. Thank God for Facebook, e-mail, and the occasional phone call, for that is usually how we cousins and Auntie Nancy still try to keep in touch. I think of every one of them so often, but the sweetest moments are those remembered from my past and that's how I can go "home" again.

"Listening to our internal music"...Each year as Californians, our lives began to have a rhythm like the cadence of a piece of music. It became like a consistent hum of comforting new rituals. As the days and months went by since we began our journey westward, we threw ourselves into multiple overlapping seasons of baseball, soccer, basketball, Orange County Song and Dance, and Show Choir. Parent meetings, tournaments, volunteer team mom, coaching, Booster Clubs, Grad Night, and lists as long as each arm carried us through, season to season. Juggling practices, rehearsals, games, meals, carpools, school work, and social activities taught everyone in our family that everything is possible with a little common sense and a lot of effort. Whew, talk about busy. Somehow we never tired of it.

Ryan and Kevin both kept up good grades, and we were so proud of their seemingly super powered efforts. Both of our sons experienced many rewards from their endeavors, and Glenn and I finally began to feel like we had made the best decision to start over and move west. There were growing pains because not everything was a success, but we had a sense of high spirits to keep on trying and learn from our mistakes. That was the ultimate priceless gift.

As the boys continued to pursue success through high school and college, they became men with different wants and needs and an agenda beyond that of our early years by their side. When they were little people, Glenn and I were their sun and moon, but now, they are each like distant stars in their own galaxies. As grown men with families of their own, I sometimes see in them a nostalgic yearning to return to the "old home town," whether here where they grew up or to Chicago where we still have relatives, to capture memories and re-connect. They still do that in their own way and style and it warms my heart.

"Notes on a successful transplant"... Now, I know you think that because I love gardening so much that I'm ready to share my secrets to a beautiful yard. Nope, this is about other aspects of nature I want to share. First, I would like to start with a quote by Ralph Waldo Emerson. "Adopt the pace of nature; Her secret is patience."

We all have the natural ability to change and adapt as nature does in such a miraculous way. I love to be awake just before dawn to see the sky turn pale, then pinkish to golden from my bedroom window. I must wait for it and experience each stage and know that dawn does come again each day in all its glory, but at it's own pace. Patience. Observe the same cadence for the stages of a glorious sunset or leaves turning color and falling in autumn and blooming flowers again in spring, reminding us that our lives are part of a natural cycle. If only we can go gracefully through our life and take our time appreciating each moment. If we have faith in natures' passages of flowers that bloom again in spring, the beauty of the change of each season, the tides of the oceans and the change from sunrise to sunset, then we know that all is as it should be. When I was transplanted from Chicago to California, the slow growth of my severed root system, as with a sturdy oak tree, took a lot of time and patience. When you see the oak tree in all its glory with a new ring of bark each year to mark growth, invisible to the eye are the roots that reach forever outward and down. I think in all of these 35 years living here, my roots must have now reached right back to Chicago and all that I left there, but are also so deep right here where I stayed. I was always able to stop to smell the roses that I love, literally. Always loving nature and learning from it and appreciating the beauty in this world were the most healing of gifts when I needed it.

"Diversions to enhance your days"... Whenever there have been gaps in my life, I would seek to discover something that that could bring me joy.

Everyone should have something to rely on to help us through stormy weather otherwise known as seasons of discontent. I love movies and television and in this era, there is so much to choose from with the invention of cable TV and Netflix. Whether a dreary day, down day, or sick day, I would be foolish not to admit how much I LOVE READING. Books and magazines were my friends from a very young age, and I'm so grateful to have had a lifetime of other worlds to enjoy and fill my mind with imagination.

I love romance novels, mysteries, and historical fiction. I am obsessed with magazines about decorating and lifestyles. Weekly trips to the library bringing home a stack of books, gave me the resources to have many moments in another world when I needed it. I always feel humble just thinking of each author struggling to find just the right words to share with their readers their innermost thoughts and visions. Each new book I read is a gift. As the reader, I always feel that even though I am a stranger, I can feel a kinship with the author and step into their mind and life just for a few moments, and I am thankful for that.

"People who need people"...I have one life to live. I realize that most of all, I have loved the people in my life. Sometimes, I fear that I have thrown out that hook and continued to reel them in too close to

me, wanting to know about their lives, what makes them happy and sad, and to share myself even though they may have needed to get off the hook at some point. I can't help myself from becoming attached and just loving them. I'm a hugger and when I see you coming, I make a beeline right up to you for a good old fashioned hug. Yeah, I know a little intense, right? Thinking of each member of my family, immediate and extended, individually and combined with all of the dear friends I have met along the years, I am so blessed. Without them, what a sad and empty existence my life might have been.

"Staring into the face of tragedy"...I must admit that in my life there have been plenty of personal problems that caused me many sleepless nights. Then out of my control, there were those traumatic events that struck fear in my heart. I can list on one hand the earthquakes that shook me to my core, and I would go to sleep with my slippers on, dressed in acceptable clothes in case of emergency. The radio turned on softly next to me, ready in case a warning needed to be heard. I threw a few pillows under the dining room table just in case of an aftershock or "the big one" when the doorways might move too far, then a short leap would get us safely under the table. Those fears faded in short time, and I would get back to

normal. As the fear dissipated, life quickly went back to a steady pace once again and I found that so amazing.

There was one event that shocked the deepest part of my heart and soul. On that day, September 11, 2001, I saw on the news the most horrifying sight I could ever imagine all within a few fateful hours. It seemed so unreal to see the sun shining on a fresh, beautiful autumn day and watch the intentional devastation come swooping down on New York, a beloved American city. I couldn't sleep for many nights after that and fell into a kind of strange deep depression to think that man was capable of such a horrible act. The stories of helping hands reaching out to strangers to assist and fire and police responders' bravery from all over risking their lives to help people to escape played over and over in my mind. My friend Mary was going to New York to visit her son the next year and asked if I wanted to join her. Glenn suggested that it might be good for me to go and visit first hand and finally put to rest some of the haunting thoughts that I just couldn't do on my own.

So there I went, and I fell in love with the city. I had heard that the people in Manhattan had changed since 9/11 and were kinder and more open than ever before. I will attest that I could feel it and see it in their eyes. They offered help without hesitation whenever I was looking at a subway map on the wall or paused to look at a street sign. It's a noisy, gritty, and crowded city, and everyone walked and used public transportation in human masses coming and going, moving on with their daily lives. There are so many languages and accents from all over the world blending into what makes the fabric that is New York. As I travelled the city streets watching the faces of the people who lived and worked in Manhattan that week, in their defense, I became so angry to think of how they all had to suffer first-hand the devastating effect of the twin towers collapse and ruin of surrounding neighborhoods that had become a ghost town, even after more than a year later.

I waited until my last day there to visit "Ground Zero." There were still ashes in the streets, and many buildings were vacant and boarded up and closed all around the blocks surrounding the site. I remembered how I had lighted commemorative candles along my front fence at home each night for a week along with some of my neighbors after that tragic day, hoping that God and his angels would see all of those little pinprick flames flickering on earth and know how we mourned. I hoped that by being at the site I might finally find healing for myself. How selfish I felt as I looked at the gaping hole of what was the twin towers and the skeleton of steel girders that still showed in places of the area's total destruction. I realized then, how long it would take the people of Manhattan to find closure, if ever at all. But then, there was the saving grace right across the street.

The little chapel that still stood. Old Saint Paul had stood there since the year 1776. It is the only building miraculously standing unharmed, but for one tree in the cemetery that was felled by falling debris. Not even the stained glass windows were broken when windows all around the neighborhood were shattered. The original roof and chandeliers were still intact as if the hands of God were placed over St. Paul's, sheltering it at the time of all total destruction around it. It became the sanctuary and meeting place for first responders during the whole tragic aftermath. They came from all over and rested their weary bodies, cried and grieved there, prayed there, were treated for injuries, ate, and rehydrated their parched, ash filled throats.

The pictorial tribute inside mourning all of the victims was so moving, but the seven foot tall wrought iron fence surrounding the four city-block property was what brought me to my knees. It was filled from top to bottom with posted photos of the missing and letters to loved ones as well as heart wrenching tributes to those who did not survive. Mothers expressed in writing such love for their children whom they would never see again in the most intimate and heartbreaking terms as only a mother had a right to share.

I was struck by reading them, that my own children may never know how I felt about them knowing that fate sometimes does not give us the opportunity to tell them. Children drew pictures to their moms and dads who would never come home again. Letters of sympathy signed by countless residents of cities from all over the world and flowers were placed at the base of the fences all around. I felt I must pay tribute and began reading them all up one block and down another only to feel uncontrolled tears flooding down my face. When sobs escaped me even though I tried to control them, I noticed others making their way around as I did and mourning as I was. I couldn't continue to the end and went back in to the chapel to pray more sincerely than I ever had before. As I left that little chapel and looked up at the hazy sun, I blew my nose a number of times, wiped my eyes, and finally I was ready to go home. Whatever in my life that I had considered a hardship dimmed to nothing following that day, and I went back home feeling so blessed.

17

The Black Lace Hanky

Grandma Carrie's threads hope and of closure

In one of her later years, on a visit to Grandma, she had me pick from her shoebox another lace trimmed hanky once again. I was married already and Grandma was having trouble seeing, so she couldn't crochet much anymore, much to her frustration. There were only two hankies left in the box, but one stood out with black thread with a little white and grey mixed in. As I looked at Grandma I thought, "She has never used this color thread before. It was such a somber tone. Perhaps her eyesight couldn't see the color." I hoped and prayed it wasn't a sign of her end days drawing near. I took that one quietly with a soft "thank you, Grandma," to her as her eyes sought out mine with a tender look. She had been ailing for a long time and a short time after that visit, she was taken to a nursing home. She passed away that September at the age of 87. Her funeral was the first loss that tore a little piece out of my heart. I held the black lace bordered hanky to wipe my tears thinking that she had probably imagined it just for this purpose as she crocheted those final threads. After that day, I washed and ironed it and put it to rest into my treasure box, only to be taken out again all too soon a few years later when my Daddy died.

Fast-forward from that time to when I was now living in California 2000 miles from home. Every time I went to visit Chicago or Mom and Dad came out here to sunny California, I always considered that it might be the last time I would see them. I knew I probably couldn't get home in time if something might happen, so I started steeling myself for that time when it would come. I still didn't expect the early morning phone call that woke me out of sleep, a raspy, distorted voice full of emotion almost shouting into the phone, "Your Dad died, so there!" I could hardly understand her, so I started asking, "Mom is this you? What happened?" And she just hung up. My sister called right back saying she was so sorry, and that she didn't know Mom was going to tell me that way. She said Mom was in shock but still insisted on calling me. "Daddy had a heart attack this morning and the ambulance just took him away. He's gone." Solid grief washed over me for the first time in my life, like a black wave. What an ugly feeling, so full of remorse and helplessness. I thought I would be so prepared. All I could think of was "Is this what grief feels like?" I felt completely numb and started to make arrangements to get the first flight home for our family, crying to the airline people on the phone.

We would always say that Polish goodbye when our phone conversations ended, or when dropping him at the airport. As children, each night we whispered those words to Mom and Dad just before we went to sleep. *Ja cie kocham, Daddy (I love you).*

I made it through the wake and funeral. Mom and Janice were so sad and tired, but being together, we eventually got back a little of our silly giggling about strange observances like the huge painting above the altar resembling the male model Fabio. We girls always had an irreverent streak of humor to call upon in times of stress like these. One look from Mom though, would be a warning, not to go too far. Others would not understand. To us, an outlet of grief and tension was always humor. We had relied on it our whole lives. We trusted each other and knew each other so well, that just one look could give us the giggles. With that blessed sense of humor and the black lace bordered hanky, I still had something to hang on to.

One memory about that difficult time was that we had left home in such a hurry, I called my best friend Joanne and said, "If I give you my key can you go over and feed the parakeet? He hasn't been eating much lately but if you can come by and give him water and seed?" Now, Joanne was the very first friend who sheltered me in her hug from the day I met her. We were kindred spirits from the first, and she knew me better than I knew myself at the time. The chain of my life had been broken, and she was the missing link that joined the two parts together again. Always willing to help and support, I called her first after the bad news of Daddy's passing and of course she agreed, wanting to help as much as she could.

When she and her husband Maury came to pick us up from the airport she said in the car, "I don't know how to tell you this, but when I went to feed the bird the day you left, he was dead at the bottom of the cage. All I could think of was how this parakeet, named Peppy after another of our childhood pets was totally mute from the day we got him. Occasionally I would hear a chirp but no matter how much all of us would try to talk to him, no response would come out of his little beak and the name Peppy began to seem foolish when you would see that little mute bird sitting silently, just staring.

When Daddy came out for a visit he would sit in the chair by the window, and that darn bird would chirp and tweet up a storm in answer to him. The two of them would whistle back and forth, and Peppy would jump from perch to swing in pure joy. When my Dad went home, he went right back to being the quiet, moody little bird. So in retrospect, I guess when Dad died, Peppy joined him in heaven. The picture of Dad with Peppy on his shoulder sitting together in heaven always made me smile. When I thought of that day, I came to realize just how much our existence here on earth is tied with so many invisible threads, as fine as the threads of Grandma Carrie's crochet, connecting us to our families, our pets, our homes. That was one instance that I noticed and appreciated that knowledge. Joanne said she buried Peppy under a bush in her yard, and I went with her to have a mini memorial service for him. Another day of mourning, but made all the easier with my good friend by my side. Joanne and I had a bond that grew stronger over the years, and we experienced many more difficult funerals together in the coming years.

Our unspoken love and faith in our friendship to each other helped us through the passing of other dear young friends from our children's high school days, most especially of Stephanie. Then both of our mothers passed away, followed by her precious daughter Allison, her husband Maury and then with Glenn, my Spanky. That black lace trimmed hanky sure got a lot of use during those years. There were so many sad goodbyes. But with each other to talk to and our inane sense of humor to lift our spirits, together we figured out ways to move on again.

18

Christmas: 2015

Fast forward to my favorite time of year. Music was once again spilling out of our home. Now, it was coming forth in our home from the computer through little powerful wireless speakers around the house. Technology has evolved. No longer a radio broadcasting a distorted sounding Christmas station from far away or 78 rpm records from the 1940's, or 33 1/3 rpm from the 1950's, or 45 rpm through the 1960's. (Interesting note, until recently I never knew that rpm meant rotations per minute). Now with a technological miracle, we had access to every Christmas favorite from even before the time our parents were little children and up to now, all played through a computer. Oh, how the century has changed.

A festive holiday season was a comforting need, especially for Glenn, who was so tired of battling his slowly failing body. We both loved to have the house all decorated, inside and out, and I hired a man to put the lights all around the outside. I brought out every bit of stored finery to decorate the tree and every nook and cranny of our house. The Christmas carols were on almost all of the time, and all of the past pain and suffering from the last year of strokes and complications with long recovery seemed to fade behind us. The potpourri pot was always simmering on the stove with spicy holiday scents. Surely it was time for a party.

On the second Saturday in December, we gathered together for a Christmas party at our house with friends and family invited. We were all laughing and eating and went out singing Christmas Carols with gusto around the block. It reminded me of the family Christmas parties from long ago that I remembered with such sweet nostalgia. John, Tom, and Chuck (Glenn's posse) decorated Glenn's walker with strings of colored Christmas lights, and they loyally walked along side of him even though he said he was feeling so good he didn't think he would need his walker. It was such a treat to see other friends we hadn't seen very often, come over to share our Christmas joy. What a great feeling! When everyone had gone home for the evening we began to turn out lights before we tucked into bed in a contented fog. Glenn commented to me with a smile, "Hon, this is the best Christmas tree and decorations ever, and the party was perfect! I loved seeing some of our friends again. It made me feel better than I have been for a long, long time. Thank you for all of your hard work." And I replied, "All of it was perfect for me too, it sure was so worth it, Sweetie," as I locked up for the night feeling so happy. Then, the last sparkling lights of the house turned off were from our beautiful Christmas tree.

19

Strength: From Her Hands To My Heart

The Black Edged Hanky Is Used Again

The next morning after the Christmas party, I found my husband Glenn in bed, deep in his final sleep. That day, all of a sudden I couldn't breathe because as I called his name to wake him there was no response, and my heart began pounding so hard. Only overwhelming silence was his response. I felt confusion, panic, and fear all at the same moment and kept trying to rouse him knowing as I called his name and patted his shoulder that he would not respond. I had tried to tell myself for weeks and months that it could be any day now, but I shouted to myself, "NOT NOW, PLEASE!" *It isn't time for him to go!* The panic in my body shot through like adrenalin from pain. His body was cold to the touch on his arms but still seemed warm on his chest or was it just my imagination? His color was already grayish.

My first impulse was to just stand there and scream. All that came out of my mouth though, was a moan of helplessness, and I began to feel the prickles of pressure behind my eyelids, while tears began to push through as I stood frozen in place. After so many years of asking him what he thought about everything, there was no answer. I remembered my questions the many times when his health took a sudden downward turn. *"What do you think Glenn? Should I call 911?"* But this time, he would not answer. I dialed it with shaking fingers and when a voice answered, I froze. My words came out in broken pieces. The operator tried to walk me through doing CPR while the paramedics were on the way, but I was trembling and couldn't follow her directions no matter how hard I tried. In my mind, I knew he did not want to be resuscitated, but I started to go through the motions anyways. In my mind, I kept repeating *always hold on, Kathie. Don't cry, because others will need you. Be strong and follow directions.*

It was Sunday morning, and Kevin would be coming in for a visit after his early morning basketball game in a couple of minutes. I half wanted him right there, but also wanted to protect him from the shock of walking in and seeing his Dad like this. *Should I pray, do I get down on my knees? Is Glenn still here watching me from above? Can he still hear me? Glenn, I need to talk to you...*

The paramedics pulled up just at the same

moment and came in to check his vitals. They knew he was gone but began to ask me questions just as Kevin came in. It is so hard to see the flash of pain on your son's face as his shoulders tensed, and I knew that I couldn't fix this biggest hurt. Almost all of my adult life, I was the fixer, soother, and helper, but at this moment, my brain was so totally numb.

The OC Sheriff came in to help and sat with me while they contacted his doctor and wrote out the report while I gave them the copy of his last wishes, and Do Not Resuscitate order. *Glenn, what should I do next?* As they finished, they gave me a brochure entitled "Grieving" along with a list of phone numbers to contact if I should need assistance.

Glenn's body had to remain here until the mortuary aides came to pick him up. The paramedics and Sheriff started to leave when my sister Janice and Sue came in with grief stricken looks on their faces. Kevin must have called Janet and she came as quick as she could make it and stayed by our side, but I got worried about this stress affecting her first pregnancy.

I thought for a moment, picturing that Glenn would not ever meet his first granddaughter and felt so sad. But with sudden clarity, I pictured him holding her while the two of them were passing in their transition between heaven and earth. Sierra waiting to be born and Glenn on the way to heaven, and they had some precious time together before they each travelled on their way. Two souls passing in the starry night. On the day she was born, when Janet and Kevin named her Sierra Glen I was sure he had already claimed her as his very own.

My oldest son Ryan, his wife Dani, and the boys weren't able to be at the Christmas party the night before, and calling them with this news grew to monstrous proportions. How that had to have hurt Ryan and Dani. I asked Kevin to call his brother Ryan, knowing that it would be especially hard for him. I just can't imagine how unfathomable the shock and pain would be for them. To Ryan and Dani, Glenn was a hero, and for Braden and Micah, their Papa was even more than that to them.

On that difficult day, LuRae and John came over followed by Zelda and Chuck. Seeing them all so heartbroken brought me a surge of fresh pain. My friends are what I refer to as my own personal trinity. Betsy, LuRae, and Zelda, in alphabetical order, are three women who have heavily influenced my later years in life. Although I have known them for oh so many years, I watched them handle careers as lifelong teachers who had a strong influence on so many young lives. They were very intelligent, verbal, dedicated, and so supportive of me. I always felt smarter when they were around and tried to absorb as much as I could from each of them. And now at this threshold of my life, they were there for me once again. I think, on this day, I was earning an F in effort because I was so numb and incoherent. I'm always so full of chatter, but today I was only able to silently talk to myself.

Why do I have to remain strong? Kathie, don't let yourself get sick with tears. Try to override your grief because it IS possible. NO, it's NOT possible! This is the worst feeling I have ever had, and I don't know what to do. Where can I just go and hide my emotions, for they are so ugly, and I know I cannot just run away.

As I sat there next to our Christmas tree remembering the beautiful night before, I mentally started turning inward. I recalled our last words to each other from the night before. His heartfelt thanks kept popping into my mind. It was a final goodbye to our lives together, unknown to each of us, but so very heart wrenching. How blessed we were to have that be our last memory together.

That morning, everyone was called by a tearful Kevin, LuRae, and all the others who tried their hardest to keep it together. I know those calls had to be so difficult for each of them.

Even thinking of it again gives me a knot in my stomach and a lump in my throat. God Bless each member of my loving family and my friends for coming so quickly because at that moment as they brokenly expressed their sorrow, my brain began to turn off.

How can I explain the numbness that invaded my thoughts and responses? *Glenn; dead.* NO, *those two words could never be together. Husband; dead.* NO, *That didn't sound right either.* Then I know it sounds crazy, but I swear to you, I felt the oddest sensation like I was ascending into the air. Not Glenn, but me. I felt like I was leaving the planet and faces blurred, sound diminished.

I felt like I was trying to catch up with him and was pulled away outside of my control. I know I was myself, but I was also Glenn; strangely the two had merged to create a shared one. Maybe we were always *one* since the day I met him, and I just never realized it.

Like I said, I was somehow not attached to earth that day. *Now, I must face each day alone. One day at a time. I don't think I can even handle that. What a disappointment I am, me, the multi-tasker.* When people asked how they could help, I just sat there like a puppet with no strings left.

I began thinking back a few weeks before, I felt that Glenn was already moving to the other side, and I wanted him to see a different doctor again even knowing it may be futile. I wanted to shift some of the responsibility to someone else. The burden was becoming too great for me.

Watching someone die slowly is something I wouldn't wish on anyone, though so many I've known have done just that. I wish that I didn't have such strong intuition, but it has gotten stronger with time. Sometimes it is painful. Some days I felt like a coward, but time and circumstance were pushing me to the breaking point. That was what our marriage was, and I lived more inside the marriage than I lived in myself for so many years. December 13th, 2015: WIDOWED.

By the close of that horrific day, the wheels were all in motion thanks to everyone who was there, Zelda had already called her son Jeff at Forest Lawn Mortuary to let him know, and they were ready for Glenn. Through the haze of that week, we worked out the details that tradition requires. Ryan, Kevin, and their wives were with me every step of the way, thank God. I don't know if I could have gotten through it any other way. The chapel was beautiful.

That Friday of the Memorial Service, we set out the photo albums that I put together each year of all the Christmases in our family from when Glenn and I were children to when we first met and up to the current year. It seemed a sweet tribute at this difficult holiday time of year to be grieving.

Kevin and Ryan put together Glenn's favorite music to be played before the service, and I wrote a eulogy to Glenn but asked the minister to read it because I knew I could not stand in front of the group and do it myself. I was only half there, I couldn't cry anymore and my face and my throat were sore from holding in my emotions. I felt frozen in time, and there was a giant lump in my throat, but I clutched the black lace edged hanky from Grandma Carrie as if my life depended on it. I felt as if she were there with me once again.

Bob the Minister had asked us many questions about our family, and he wanted to get to know all about Glenn and our whole family before he spoke in front of the congregation. That day, when he shared with the audience that Glenn was a musician and played the accordion, everyone's eyes in the whole chapel including ours shot up in surprise. Afterward, we heard many comments from friends with a little smile. "Gosh, we never knew that Glenn was an accordion player!" I think Glenn's eyes would have shot up in surprise as well, but he would have gotten a laugh out of that one. When Glenn was a teenager, he drove his sister Linda to accordion practices and performances every week and he never played, but that small error was just the little ice breaker that we all needed, a little comic relief.

It felt so strange to see faces and not be able to connect to names, but I still tried to greet them. It was easier to simply sit silently. Dani, Ryan's wife, helped her mother Maria Elena set up at our house for after the memorial service. She arranged to have food for everyone after the memorial service.

Janet's Mom and Dad helped cover the costs. I can't remember any more of it. For the first time in my whole life, I was not in control of one single thing, not even myself. I only remember sitting in the living room and hearing kind condolences. I wonder, does the brain shut down like that as part of God's plan to get us through it? Is that nature's way of beginning the healing process? I only knew I was not in control of any of it, and I had to ride across it like a boat without oars on the waves of the ocean. Adrift is the only word that I can use to explain it.

The family came over the next day, my dear nephew Scott and his wife Katie came over with Ryan and Kevin and their families. We all had stood together in Glenn's last bad year as the sturdiest support system. The three boys Ryan, Kevin, and Scott were each pallbearers along with Glenn's closest friends John, Chuck, and Tom.

The boys were recalling some things of the day before, and they brought up an unusual experience to share with me. I just could not attend the lowering of the casket, and I knew Glenn would understand. I set out for home, and the guys stayed to finish the burial.

Ryan, Kevin, and Scott were sitting in their car waiting to drive to the gravesite. They were wondering what was taking the attendants so long to come out from closing the mortuary. The hearse was parked directly in front of them with Glenn safely tucked in his casket, with our mementos within, right in front of them. All of a sudden, the brake lights of the hearse both went on and it jolted slightly as if someone was going to shift gears and drive. The guys said to each other, "Finally, now we can get going." The brake lights went off again and they sighed, "Nope, I guess not."

Then the brake lights went on again and off, but they noticed two mortuary assistants come out and they got in the front seat of the car. Ryan, Kevin and Scott sat and stared ahead of them and one said, "Did you just see what I saw?" They all looked at each other and said, "Did those brake lights go on and off with no one in the hearse, or was it my imagination?" No way, they all saw it. "Maybe there was a man in the car already waiting for the other two." When they pulled up to the gravesite, only the same two mortuary assistants get out and Ryan, Kevin, and Scott looked at each other and then asked the mortuary assistants if there was a third man in the hearse before. The answer was no, just the two who had been in the chapel while our boys were waiting. As they later shared that story of a strange and difficult day, I explained to them that Glenn was angriest and most frustrated about the fact that he could no longer drive and for the last years argued for that privilege whenever he could, even beyond our best advice. He missed driving so much; I think that he took his last opportunity to get behind the wheel once again, one last time. The universe is a mysterious place, and that was one story we will probably never know the answer to but it sure does give us pause for thought. *Spanky behind the wheel for one last drive.*

Glenn and I were bequeathed both our son's cast off cellular flip phones from their high school days. They convinced us that it was time to get used to the new technology. Grudgingly, we took them with us but pretty much only used them for emergencies. We used them very sparingly. The day after the funeral, I was looking around for my cell phone, thinking I misplaced it once again as I was prone to do. The boys kept trying to call it and try to find it for me. I couldn't find Glenn's cell phone either, and we also kept calling it trying to hear if it was ringing under a cushion or under a pile of clothes. No luck! They asked me to think back to where I had used them or seen them last, and I would eventually find it.

The last place I saw the phones was when I set them on the dining room table to put in my purse. At the time, I was gathering precious mementoes to enclose in the casket with Glenn. Included in the stack on the table were drawings made by Micah and Braden for their Papa, photos of the family and the rosary beads from his father's funeral, a fresh flower from our rose bushes, Cubs and other Chicago memorabilia, and a sonogram copy of Sierra Glen (named after Papa) his first granddaughter soon to be born.

Anyways, I suddenly recalled that just before the funeral we looked at the clock and everyone suddenly said, "We're going to be late! Get that stuff in the bag. Let's get going, and we'll give it to the mortuary assistant." So I swiped the contents of the table into the bag and handed it over. My job was done.

Not only mine, but Glenn's cell phone were in the bag that got buried in the coffin with him. Flip phones, Rest In Peace. I laughed with the family later about how the consistent cell phones ringing coming from the ground must have startled people walking or working in the cemetery. The boys said it was a sign from Glenn that it was time for a smart phone, so that's where I headed the next day. The clerk at the Verizon store found my story about how my flip phones were lost quite unusual. Another last joke from beyond.

Glenn was the type of man who deserved to be remembered with the same love and affection he felt for his family and friends. He could be very stubborn in his ways, but was a humble man. He was an avid sports fan, especially his beloved Chicago Cubs baseball team. He enjoyed his son's multitude of sports games and helped whenever he could whether by coaching baseball, practicing soccer with them, or being the Basketball Booster Club President.

Glenn and I were both so extremely proud of all of the hard work and effort Ryan and Kevin made as they moved up each year, but Glenn was over the moon at what they achieved. In our eyes, our sons were always "Super Stars."

To say that Glenn as a spiritual man in his own style was a very apt description. He prayed every day. He felt that his recovery from alcoholism is attributed to divine intervention, and he was always grateful for that. During the many years of his six major surgeries complicated with paralysis, massive infections, and necrosis, then followed by three strokes, he continued to pray for strength to get through it all. He prayed for his sons and his family every night to St. Jude, helper and keeper of the hopeless and felt that St. Jude certainly was his own personal patron saint. Glenn was a proud man but compassionate.

He was so loyal and loving, and he had a work ethic like no other. He loved his co-workers and considered them his extended family and never wanted to let them down. He was determined to return to work after every surgery and medical malady until the strokes finally felled him like an old oak tree. It was then that he finally gave in. Since he has been gone, we have all had a very difficult time adjusting and missing him. As for me, I simply loved him. His headstone reads:

Glenn Robert Staniec
"Chicago's Son"
1948 – 2015

Cherished husband and father. Devoted son, brother and uncle. Adoring papa and faithful friend...beloved by all. To live in the hearts of those we love is never to die.

Each day from the moment he passed away and on for many months, I swam back to the surface for air. Pulling myself back to earth one bit at a time. Why does it feel so painful? It's like being born again as an infant, and I feel like I have to learn everything all over again. Do all married women feel that way when they lose their husbands? I guess I can consider myself lucky, for in a way we had almost 50 years to understand and finally accept one another and still love unconditionally. Glenn was either sick or in pain or recuperating for so many years, maybe 15 or so altogether. We had time to heal any hurts and continued to learn to love under the worst circumstances. He was never a complainer, but the quality of his life and mine became so limited especially toward the end. Sometimes I felt cheated, but most of the time I felt sorry for him and admired his strength and persistence to keep on trying to heal and get better. His bravery was so much more apparent than mine. We had time and space to grow together during his disability. I could never let him go through what he did alone, because I knew he might not make it. Choice was not a word that fit into either of our vocabularies. *Responsibility to each other* were our chosen words, and we chose that and all of the love that grew because of it.

> *"...To have and to hold from this day forward, for better for worse, for richer or for poorer, in sickness and in health, to love and to cherish, 'til death do us part."*

I can still recall those words we repeated to each other in our youthful, tentative voices on our wedding day so long ago. It all went back to our vows, and we had passed the test of time.

20

Finally

At first, some days after Glenn passed away, I could barely get out of bed, but that got easier as each month went by. I went to see a psychologist and attended some grief counseling sessions. I was determined to do everything to help myself recover and continue living life and enjoy it again. Then after one group I tried, I became a Grief Group dropout and finally felt that I had moved on, essentially on a more comfortable path. As I am completing my memoir, I realize I am finally piecing together all the puzzle pieces that have made up my life. The most comforting fact is that in looking back, I can see more fully who I really am now. I think I was afraid to look too closely at myself because I would not like what I may see.

I have come to realize that there is a gift that we're given later in life if we should choose to receive it. Parts of our physical body start to slow down and fail and that is so darn frustrating, but the knowledge and understanding of life is intensified and comes into much sharper focus to balance that.

In my most recent years, my beloved sister and our dearest friend Sue, who is a sister to us now, also picked up their roots and moved here. In the first stage of her story, my sister Janice, still living in Chicago suburbs, said a tearful goodbye as her two sons moved to California to make a fresh start one after another. Then, shortly after Janice and Sue followed their trail westward. As I observed each in their move from one lifetime to another, I was reminded of my own struggles and saw that they were experiencing their own metamorphosis as I did.

Having them with me was a precious gift just at a time when I sorely needed it, because Glenn had entered into his final and most serious stages of his illness. It was as if their moves here were already predestined to happen. But once again, they each had to discover where their roots were to reach outward to. Most recently, when both of my sister's sons moved back to Illinois with their newfound loves, Jan and Sue moved to Henderson, Nevada.

When my oldest son Ryan decided to move to Texas with Dani, Micah and Braden, I was struck with the painful memory of driving away from my parents that day in Chicago. The old saying kept running through my mind, *"What goes around, comes around."* It took all of my newfound confidence and a stern talk with myself to accept their move and put my realization into practice.

We had survived our California transition to a new life and we were better people for it. Over and over again, I have been reminded of Grandma Carrie's story. She never knew what was on the next horizon, but she continued to seek happiness and thrive as best she could. I am beginning to wonder if there is still some new growth on my own horizon. Father Time and Mother Nature surely work in mysterious ways.

As I complete my memoir, I can see the turning point of my life was when I began my journey west. I was unsure of myself and felt like I was abandoned in all aspects. I was on the "pity pot." Poor me, all alone, orphaned, alienated from everything I knew and loved. My husband and sons had only me to make things right. No more grandparents to turn to for a helping hand. I didn't know if I would fit in. I didn't know if I could love it here as I had loved what I left behind or find friends to cherish. I was unsure if Glenn and I would be able to overcome the challenges together or if it would break us apart.

As an analogy, it was no joke to say that in earthquake country I was on really unstable ground in relation to my whole life. As it turns out, I found my whole life here. All I ever wanted and so many things I didn't know I wanted. So, it has become easier to know and accept myself after all these years. I'm not afraid anymore. I have stood strong.

Each day, I'm still changing. For now, life is good and everything else in coming years will be the cherry with sprinkles on top. I am wealthy beyond imagination. Not wealth in the sense of lots of money, but in my heart. I have a treasure trove of memories. Also in a drawer of my dresser, I have a precious box of hankies with beautiful lace borders of every color to remind me of my heritage. Each one represents another stage of my life and my connection to my family.

In the accounting of my life, I have had parents and a sister who nurtured me and created a nest for me in a world so beautiful, yet so complex and frustrating. My move to California nudged me out of the safety of that nest to finally fly on my own. I have had romance and the love of my life to walk beside me through all of the hills and valleys. The hardest situations made me stronger in the end.

Recently, I began a Bucket List and started to cross things off one by one. A trip to Paris on a riverboat cruise with my friend Joanne was a big one. We also visited good friends, Carolyn and Taylor in Franklin, Tennessee, outside of Nashville. That was a lovely change of pace for us. I started taking Line Dance classes, joined an ukulele group, tried art classes, and signed up for classes at Long Beach State in areas of my interest. I loved the Arts and Crafts design class and especially, Memoir Writing 101.

That class was the one that got me on the path of getting started writing this. I stood in front of the group at the podium, adjusted the microphone, and began to read the first few chapters to my fellow students and unexpectedly, I started to cry. So much had been buried inside of me for so many years. What an embarrassment that was, but when finished with what I had started and the group applauded, I knew I had to complete it. That gave me the courage to be brave. My son Kevin kept me going with his advice and support all the way through. Gosh, I must be getting sentimental in my old age because his recent call with a bold, "Congratulations, Mom! You did a great job on your book!" It actually brought some tears to my eyes again knowing I had finally done it.

In choosing the title of this chapter "Finally," I can't resist adding a little note of closure regarding something special from 2016. For generations, everyone in our family has always been the most loyal of Cubs fans.

While growing up, Glenn and I listened to our parents cheer "our team" through each season. Each year when the Cubbies didn't make it to the World Series, in undertones they would always remark, "Tough break, but, for sure, next year." Every dad, son, and even their mothers had a Cubs cap to wear until threadbare. Our dad's went to their graves never seeing that WIN happen, and the seasons flowed swiftly by. But each year, tradition had families keeping in touch with each other on the finer points of the game. Glenn and his dear sister Linda, would call each other long distance after each game to discuss what they could have or should have done to win. Ryan and Kevin checked in with Glenn with comments after each game suggesting what would have worked better. There is something about Cubs fans and Chicagoans that is so heartwarming. They are fans *forever*, win or lose. The Cubs motto is "We never quit!" And their fans at the hallowed ivy walls of Wrigley don't ever lose faith in their team.

Then came 2016 after Glenn was newly departed. Sierra, our first granddaughter had her blue Cubs cap with red sequins honoring that familiar "C" and sat with her cousins Micah, Braden, and Harrison with their caps sitting squarely in the rally position on their heads, watching the games together with all of us. It just couldn't come easy, couldn't be won without extra drama. The Cubs had a chance to win the World Series for the first time since 1908. That's one hundred and eight years of *"try, try again."* Ryan had placed a "W" flag (a Cubbie blue W on white ground for WIN) on Glenn's grave while thousands of other graves were marked with that and other Cubs Memorabilia all over the country. Every game became a family affair, and then came that last one when the Cubs carried a 6-3 lead into the eighth inning, six outs away from a cathartic victory. But a double and a two-run home run by the Indians wiped out that lead and *tied the game*. The deadlock held through the ninth inning. We had a sinking feeling, but we all were sure that those departed souls of our grandfathers and fathers with Glenn right there in the front were angels in the outfield. Many silent prayers were sent out to them. Then the rain came, of course. *Thank you, Glenn.* The top of the 10th inning was delayed for about 15 minutes by a deluge. Totally unexpected and so mystical as if God said, *"Come on guys, we got your fans out here in heaven helping and sent the rain to let you get it together, play ball now!"*

I'm sure those 25 guys on the team had more help than we could see. Once that rain let up, the Cubs poured it on in the 10th inning, scoring 2 runs to provide the cushion they needed. I am *positive* Glenn, Stony, Casey, and all those other departed Cubs fans were there to cheer as we all did. In those moments after the "WIN" quite a few happy souls, both living and departed shared their joy. How fragile and thin the veil is between heaven and earth.

Now, for a final little review of things of most value in my life. I have been so blessed by my handsome, witty, caring sons of whom I have always been so proud. More precious than gold doesn't even touch on the feelings I hold in my heart for each of them. They have enchanted me as tiny babies and made me so proud as grown men. I love them completely but when it comes to my children, there just aren't enough words that seem to express what I feel inside. They have given me gifts beyond anything I ever imagined and have filled every corner of my heart.

In both of my daughters-in-law, I have placed my trust and I love them both. They are patient and loving to me, even on days that I babbled and tried too hard and drove them a little crazy. They adore their children, and they love my sons and support them in everything and for that, I'll be eternally appreciative.

Those two women are made of very strong stuff. It gives me a feeling of such comfort to think that these women will also continue the journey of Carrie, Sunny, and of me into the future. We have walked that same path and have had so many fears and regrets, but we were blessed with much joy and hope to help balance that. Now my sons wives will have to continue on their own journey that is still just beginning. I have confidence that both of them will stand strong and be proud of who they are and grow to understand who they will still become.

I gave one of Grandma's lace bordered hankies to each of them on the day before they married my sons. I gave it as a gift from my heart and also from my mothers' and my grandmother's heart with so much love. I wonder if Grandma Carrie ever thought of just how special her delicate lace would be some 60 years later when given to each new bride as I hugged her on the eve of her wedding day.

I hope and pray that someday each of them will share our story and give it to her son's new bride or to her own daughter passing on our love to another strong and beautiful woman to inspire courage into her own personal journey through life.

Each of my grandchildren are the purest examples of what it means to give and receive unconditional love, no strings attached. God certainly knew what he was doing to plan for us this precious gift of grandchildren. There could be no better example of the miracle of life, and as I get older, and I begin to reach "The Autumn Of My Life" as Frank Sinatra used to sing, these little babies have brought me total joy. What never ceases to amaze me is their resilience and how I can see traits inherited from their ancestors already becoming apparent. Through them I define innocence, happiness, and love come full circle.

What a wonderful feeling to watch them grow and to hear their laughter. I have been blessed beyond measure!

When I look at photographs of myself, I study each picture. Sometimes I look at the face and think, "who is that person?" Other times, I want to blacken out my face with a pencil or cut me out of the corner of the shot, but I don't. I am who I am, the good and the bad of me. I was born, grew up, married, and had two sons. But what did I have to show for my years? Who will be left to remember me? By writing this memoir, I wanted to leave a legacy of my grandmother's and my mother's life and weave it into my own life, so there will also be a tribute to them to carry forward. For all our strengths and shortcomings, we each loved intensely and for that, we hope to be remembered best.

So, this is the story of my life and the lives that brought me here. Those in particular were strong, resilient, and creative women. They were the foundation of our family I have known well and been inspired by, my grandmother Carrie, my mother Sunny, and the Happel sisters.

Their stories began long ago and in places very far away, but to me they are the threads that have been crocheted into the strong pattern of what I have made of my life. I am contented and feel fulfilled, and that is the most precious gift of all.

For just a moment, imagine we are sitting on the two rockers on my front porch of the home that I have come to love so dearly. It is far from that little house on Argyle Street where my first memories began. This home of mine is full of so many memories, both beautiful and sad, but fertile ground for my own personal growth and my remembrances of days gone by. Come closer and pull your chair next to mine.

From my rocking chair I have read, daydreamed, and cried. I have rocked my first grandson singing softly to him and each precious baby that came after. I listened to the birds' sweet song and watched the world go by. It's certainly not the apple orchard of my childhood, but still one of my favorite places. It has been my haven in the true sense of the word. Listen, can you hear the breeze rustle the leaves?

The scent of sweet nature is all around me. I feel the air growing cooler as the day comes to a close, but the rays of the sun are still warm on my hands. These hands, like those of my mother and her mother before her.

A Note From The Author

As you may have noticed, my memoir is primarily about what I have inherited from the women in my life and what a strong influence they have had on me. My intentions are certainly not to leave out the men whom I have loved and been inspired by. I am so very thankful for their part in my life. Without them my life would have been like a crossword puzzle without clues, or salt without pepper. Men and women need each other to learn how to have balance in life. I have inherited much from my father who has remained a steadfast figure in all my memories. Of course, I've been influenced in many ways by my sons and grandsons. I have learned so many important lessons because of them and have so many more stories to tell, but to share all those thoughts and memories would fill another volume just by itself. So, in parting, let me just say, "To be continued..."

Dedication

To the women in my life, past and present, both friends and family. Each have walked through the many hills and valleys of life and still managed to come out stronger. In my heart, they are always beside me, inspiring me to do the same. In particular, I dedicate this memoir to my sister Janice Mary who knows me better and has known me longer than anyone else on earth and still loves me for who I am. That feeling is mutual, Sis.

Made in the USA
Middletown, DE
20 September 2020